T0323694

Cambridge Elements ≡

Elements in the Problems of God
edited by
Michael L. Peterson
Asbury Theological Seminary

ORTHODOXY AND HERESY

Steven Nemes
North Phoenix Preparatory Academy

CAMBRIDGE
UNIVERSITY PRESS

Shaftesbury Road, Cambridge CB2 8EA, United Kingdom

One Liberty Plaza, 20th Floor, New York, NY 10006, USA

477 Williamstown Road, Port Melbourne, VIC 3207, Australia

314–321, 3rd Floor, Plot 3, Splendor Forum, Jasola District Centre,
New Delhi – 110025, India

103 Penang Road, #05–06/07, Visioncrest Commercial, Singapore 238467

Cambridge University Press is part of Cambridge University Press & Assessment,
a department of the University of Cambridge.

We share the University's mission to contribute to society through the pursuit of
education, learning and research at the highest international levels of excellence.

www.cambridge.org
Information on this title: www.cambridge.org/9781009268172

DOI: 10.1017/9781009268189

First published 2022

A catalogue record for this publication is available from the British Library.

ISBN 978-1-009-26817-2 Paperback
ISSN 2754-8724 (online)
ISSN 2754-8716 (print)

Orthodoxy and Heresy

Elements in the Problems of God

DOI: 10.1017/9781009268189
First published online: October 2022

Steven Nemes
North Phoenix Preparatory Academy

Author for correspondence: Steven Nemes, snemes2@gmail.com

Abstract: "Orthodoxy" and "heresy" are essential categories by which the "catholic" theological tradition evaluates the (im)propriety of various beliefs and practices relative to its nonnegotiable commitments. This Element sketches moments in the development of Christian orthodoxy and heresy in time, as much in the Old and New Testaments as in the history of the Church. It also touches on the vexed theological-methodological question of the relation between scripture and ecclesial tradition before concluding with a critique of the "catholic" tradition's preoccupation with orthodoxy and heresy in favor of a Christian theology "without anathemas" that is concerned only with truth.

Keywords: orthodoxy and heresy, theological method, theology without anathemas, systematic theology, scripture and tradition

ISBNs: 9781009268172 (PB), 9781009268189 (OC)
ISSNs: 2754-8724 (online), 2754-8716 (print)

Contents

1 A Formal Analysis of the Concepts

The concern of this section is to propose a formal analysis of the concepts of orthodoxy and heresy. The discussion begins with a consideration of the possible meanings of these terms in relation to each other according to their Greek etymology. Then these concepts are situated within the wider framework of the ways of relating to things that are constitutive of Christian life as such, namely belief-that, belief-in, and living-with. The discussion terminates by raising the question of truth and of what orthodoxy and heresy have to do with possessing it. This question remains in the background in Sections 2–4 and is brought to the fore once more in Section 5.

1.1 "Orthodoxy" and "Heresy"

The words "orthodoxy" and "heresy" are both of Greek origin. A consideration of their respective etymologies helps reveal their possible meanings and the relations that obtain between them (Liddell and Scott 1996: 41, 444, 1249).

"Orthodoxy" comes from the Greek word *orthodoxia*, which is itself a compound of two terms: *orthos* and *doxa*. *Orthos* is an adjective that means straight or upright. By extension, it means right, safe, true, or correct. It is in this extended sense that *orthos* becomes an evaluative term with a positive connotation. To say that something is *orthos* is to say that it is somehow good or right. *Doxa* has two principal meanings that are of concern for present purposes. In typically Hellenic contexts, it can mean opinion, notion, or judgment. *Doxa* in this sense refers to an attitude taken toward a proposition. Alternatively phrased, *doxa* can refer to the propositional or hermeneutic attitude taken toward something. To have a *doxa* in this sense is to think or say that something is of such and such a quality or nature. In Hebraic contexts, however, it more commonly denotes glory or splendor. In this sense, the term refers to the imposing manifestation of a thing in experience. This is the meaning in Exod. 16:10 LXX, which says that the "glory of the Lord" (*hē doxa Kuriou*) covered Aaron in a cloud. Matt. 4:8 likewise recounts how Christ is taken during His temptations to a high place from which He can see all the kingdoms of the earth and "their splendor" (*tēn doxan autōn*). The *doxa* of a thing would be the power with which it imposes itself in experience. This duality of meanings of *doxa* according to context also applies to the related verb *doxazō*. In Hellenic contexts, this can refer to thinking, imagining, supposing, or holding an opinion. In the Hebraic context, it especially means to magnify or extol. Thus in Exod. 15:2 LXX the Hebrews sing after their liberation from Egypt: "He is my God, and I will extol (*doxasō*) Him." In the same way, Paul writes in Rom. 1:21 that the idolatrous Gentiles did not worship God as God (*ouch hōs theon edoxasan*).

And John 7:39 affirms that the Holy Spirit "was not" while Jesus was not yet glorified (*Iēsous oudepō edoxasthē*).

Orthodoxia thus can be taken in at least two senses, depending on the interpretation of *doxa*. If one opts for the meaning more prevalent in Hellenic contexts, *orthodoxia* comes to refer to right or proper belief. Aristotle refers to this idea without using the precise term in *Nicomachean Ethics* VI, 9, when he writes that truth or *alētheia* is *doxēs orthotēs*: "correctness of opinion" (1142b11). On the other hand, if one interprets *doxa* as exaltation or magnification, then *orthodoxia* refers to proper worship of God. And if one considers holding proper beliefs as a constituent element of worship, then the two senses of *orthodoxia* blend together.

"Heresy" comes from the Greek word *hairesis*, but the connection from the Greek original term to the English theological term is indirect. *Hairesis* principally means taking – for example, the taking of a town by some foreign ruler. As derived from the verb *haireomai*, it means choice. The connection of these senses is obvious insofar as everything one takes is something one chooses for oneself. Lev. 22:18 LXX thus speaks of the gifts to be offered by any man of the children of Israel or by any stranger "according to all their choice" (*kata pasan hairesin autōn*). Closely related to this is the meaning of purpose or course of action. And from this is derived the meaning of sect, school, and religious party. *Hairesis* in this sense refers to a collection of persons who have chosen for themselves a particular way of living and of thinking about things.

Hairesis – much like the English word "sect" – can also be taken as a neutral or negative term. Understood neutrally, *hairesis* calls to mind the fact that not all persons are born into the same way of life. Human beings find themselves in the situation of having to make choices about what to think and how to lead their lives. There is no "default" life for humanity. Every *hairesis* in this neutral sense of "sect" thus constitutes a possible way in which a person may choose for him- or herself to live. Acts 5:17 speaks in this sense of the "sect of the Sadducees" (*hē ousa hairesis tōn Saddoukaiōn*) and at 15:5 of "some of the sect of the Pharisees" (*tines tōn apo tēs haireseis tōn Pharisaiōn*). Acts 24:5 likewise contains a reference to Christians as "the sect of the Nazarenes" (*tēs tōn Nazōraiōn haireseis*). Sadduceeism, Pharisaism, and Christianity as *haireseis* thus represent religious choices in the first-century Palestinian context.

From the perspective of a person who has already assumed a particular sect, more specifically for whom there cannot in fact be any freedom of choice about some matter, *hairesis* can take on the negative sense of heresy. Those things with respect to which it is considered that there can be no choice to live or think differently become possible objects of heresy. It is in something like this negative sense that the apostle Paul lists "factions" (*haireseis*) at Gal. 5:20 as the effects of the flesh that exclude from the kingdom of God. And 2 Pet. 2:1 likewise warns of the forthcoming appearance of false prophets and teachers who will bring "destructive heresies" (*haireseis apōleias*) into the church. To the extent that involves choosing to live or think in a certain way where there is in fact no freedom to choose, *hairesis* as heresy becomes a manifestation of a certain perversity of spirit. Thus Tertullian notes that the apostle Paul at Tit. 3:10–11 calls the *hairetikon anthrōpon* or "heretical man" self-condemned "because he has himself chosen that for which he is condemned" (*Prescription against the Heretics* 6).

On the basis of these etymological and semantic considerations, it is now possible to appreciate the relationship between *orthodoxia* and *hairesis*. Understood in the neutral sense, every *hairesis* or sect is one possible way among many of living and thinking about things. As long as one is still not committed to any particular sect, there would apparently be for one as yet no such thing as *orthodoxia*. The distinction between proper and improper ways of thinking and of worshiping God can only arise for a person to the extent that he or she has already committed him- or herself to a particular way of living and thinking. This means that every sect or *hairesis* in the neutral sense can become a heresy or *hairesis* in the negative sense only after one has made a choice, whether implicitly or explicitly, among the many possible options. One man's orthodoxy is another man's heresy insofar as the judgment of heresy presupposes a prior standard of orthodoxy. Only after one has decided in favor of a particular *hairesis* – that is, a sect for which there is in fact no freedom of choice about some matter – do alternative *haireseis* that see things differently become heresies.

These brief considerations should suffice for the illustration of the conceptual interrelationship between *orthodoxia* and *hairesis* considered in themselves. It will now be well to consider further the relation between these concepts once situated within the framework of relations that are constitutive of Christian life.

1.2 Belief-That, Belief-In, and Living-With

Being a Christian is a matter of being related in certain ways to external realities. For present purposes, three specific ways of relating to things are especially important: belief-that, belief-in, and living-with.

Belief-that can be variously characterized. One way of understanding it is to say that it is a matter of being related in a certain way toward a proposition. One can also say that it is a way of relating propositionally toward the world of things. It can be understood as a matter of assenting to the truth of some statement, of saying "Yes" in one's mind to what another proposes for belief, or it can be understood as adopting a certain interpretation of reality. In any case, the idea is that being a Christian is a matter of believing-that various statements are true – that is, believing-that things are a certain way. For example, one can believe-that God exists or else believe about God that He exists.

In the earliest days of the church, those beliefs-that that were taken as essentially constitutive of apostolic Christianity were called by some authors the *regula fidei*, the "rule of faith." Not all statements of this rule were identical. Among these beliefs-that constituting the rule of faith, Tertullian mentions the belief-that "there is but one God, the Selfsame with the Creator of the world, Who produced all things out of nothing through His Word sent down in the beginning of all things" (*Prescription against the Heretics* 13). Origen of Alexandria too claims that "the holy apostles, in preaching the faith of Christ, delivered with utmost clarity to all believers . . . certain points that they believed to be necessary," including the idea that "this just and good God, the Father of our Lord Jesus Christ, himself gave the law and the prophets and the Gospels, who is also the God of the apostles and of the Old and New Testaments" (*On First Principles* Preface 3–4). And this is of course only a small sampling of the essential apostolic teaching as these figures understood it.

Belief-that can thus be understood either as a relation to a proposition or a propositional way of relating toward the world of things. But alongside belief-that, there is also belief-in. This is not principally a relation toward a proposition but rather to a person or community of persons. Believing-in is a matter of committing and entrusting oneself to another. Whereas belief-that can be understood as a relation toward a proposition, or else as a way of relating propositionally toward items in the world, belief-in is a way of orienting oneself toward another. These are very different things, as Jas 2:19 appreciates: "You believe that God is one; you do well. Even the demons believe – and shudder." The demons also believe-that certain things are true about God, but they do not believe-in God in the way that they should as His creatures. They lack the appropriate orientation of the heart toward their Creator. Karl Barth describes well this sort of "personal orientation." "Faith is the orientation of man on Jesus Christ. It is faith in Him. The man who believes looks to Him, holds to Him, and depends on Him" (Barth 1956: 743). Being a Christian is consequently not only a matter of believing-that various things are the case but also of believing-in God and in Jesus.

The precise relation between belief-that and belief-in for Christian life is disputable (cf. O'Collins 2011: 167). It is possible to believe-in a person without having very particular beliefs-that with respect to him or her. Children believe-in their parents and entrust themselves to their fathers and mothers without knowing very much about their personal histories or having a philosophically robust understanding of the metaphysics of human beings. But it would seem impossible to believe-in a person without at the same time implicitly or explicitly possessing at least very general beliefs-that this person is reliable or has good intentions and so on. It can also be debated whether the failure to possess certain beliefs-that disorients one's belief-in to such an extent that one no longer believes-in the same person or community as others who believe-that differently. One might thus wonder whether a person who believes-that Jesus is not divine can be said to believe-in the same Jesus as one who does affirm His divinity (see Nemes 2021b).

In addition to belief-that and belief-in, a third relation constitutive of Christian life is living-with. This is also a nonpropositional relation to a person or a community of persons. Living-with means sharing one's life with another in such a way as to interact regularly and to have an overlapping set of concerns. Living-with can generally be positive or negative. Friends live-with one another in a positive way while enemies live-with one another in a negative way. A friend is a person one would like to live-with whereas an enemy is a person one would strictly prefer to live-without. But for present purposes, living-with should be taken in the positive sense.

Christians live-with each other in what can be called the communion or fellowship (*koinōnia*) of the church. This practice originated in the very beginnings of the movement. After the resurrection and ascension of Jesus, the apostles gathered in Jerusalem in a house where they were staying, "constantly devoting themselves to prayer, together with certain women, including Mary the mother of Jesus, as well as His brothers" (Acts 1:12–14). It is there that Peter and the rest make the decision to replace Judas with Matthias after casting lots (1:15–26). Luke also writes that "When the day of Pentecost had come, they were all together in one place" (2:1). Upon the preaching of Peter and the conversion of the crowds, the community of Christians was expanded. The new converts who were baptized "devoted themselves to the apostles' teaching and fellowship, to the breaking of bread and the prayers" (2:42). The earliest Christians lived-with each other in the sense described earlier: "All who believed were together and had all things in common" (2:44). They prayed for each other (1 Thess. 1:2) and also asked each other for prayer (Eph. 6:19). They admonished one another when they did not consider that they were living up to the demands of the truth, as Paul recounts doing with Peter (Gal. 2:11–14). They gathered to worship God and to celebrate the Lord's Supper (cf. 1 Cor. 11:20–21). And these various modes of living-with that are constitutive of Christian life as such continue to the present.

In addition to living-with each other, Christians also live-with God in Jesus through the Holy Spirit. To say that Christians live-with God is to say that their lives are led "before God" (*coram Deo*) or with an awareness of God. The apostle Paul is recorded in Acts 23:1 as saying to the council, "Brothers, up to this day I have lived with a clear conscience before God." What makes Christian faith distinctly Christian as opposed to generically theistic is that it is a living-with God that takes place through the mediation of Jesus. Thus Paul writes in 1 Cor. 1:9 that "God is faithful; by Him you were called into the fellowship of His Son, Jesus Christ our Lord." First John 1:3 communicates the basic invitation of the college of the apostles. "We declare to you what we have seen and heard so that you also may have fellowship with us; and truly our fellowship is with the Father and with His Son Jesus Christ." And John says later that "No one who denies the Son has the Father; everyone who confesses the Son has the Father also" (2:23). This conception of things is drawn from Jesus's own words about Himself. He is recorded at John 14:6 as saying, "I am the way, the truth, and the life. No one comes to the Father except through me." And at Matt. 11:27 He says, "All things have been handed over to me by my Father, and no one knows the Son except the Father, and no one knows the Father except the Son and anyone to whom the Son chooses to reveal Him." Thus, according to the Christian conception of things, Christian life-with God is a matter of being welcomed into the circle of fellowship of the Father and the Son through the invitation of this Son Himself and of His followers.

Part of Christian living-with God is offering oneself to Him. The apostle Paul at Rom. 12:1 calls Christians to "present your bodies as a living sacrifice, holy and acceptable to God, which is your spiritual worship." This self-offering is effectively obedience to the example of Jesus Himself, who according to Heb. 9:14 "through the eternal Spirit offered Himself without blemish to God" as a sacrifice for the sins of the whole world. And 1 Tim. 2:5–6 writes of Jesus that He is the "one mediator between God and humankind . . . who gave Himself as a ransom for all." There is of course a difference between Jesus's self-offering and the self-offering of Christians who live-with God. Jesus offers Himself to God on behalf of others in order to make atonement for their sins. But by offering Himself for others, He also calls these others into friendship with Himself and His Father. The self-offering to the Father on behalf of others is a part of the greater outreach of God to human beings. This means that every Christian offers him- or herself to God simply out of love for God and obedience to Him in response to this invitation to friendship. This is the sense of the teaching at 2 Cor. 5:19 that "in Christ God was reconciling the world to Himself, not counting their trespasses against them."

Christian life thus consists in these relations. It is a matter of believing-that this or that is true – for example, the things enumerated as constituting the *regula fidei* by Tertullian or Origen. It is also a matter of believing-in God and

Jesus. This is not principally a matter of being related toward a proposition (or, alternatively, of being propositionally related toward the world) but rather of having a certain orientation of the heart toward another. Finally, being a Christian is also a matter of living-with other Christians as well as living-with God through Jesus Christ in the Holy Spirit. Many more things could have been said about this; for example, Christians also live-with their enemies in a certain way, namely by praying for them and returning good for evil (Matt. 5:43–48).

It is now possible to ask how the theological categories of *orthodoxia* and *hairesis* are understood with reference to the relations of belief-that, belief-in, and living-with that constitute Christian existence as such. *Orthodoxia* refers to *doxa* that is *orthē*. If *doxa* is understood to refer to opinion or judgment, then orthodoxy is a matter of believing the proper things. If *doxa* is taken in the sense of exaltation or worship, then orthodoxy refers to a proper way of believing-in and living-with God. If *hairesis* is understood in the negative sense of heresy, it refers either to a way of believing-that or believing-in or living-with that is considered by some persons fundamentally to compromise the integrity of the way of thinking and living to which every Christian is called. And if holding to proper beliefs-that is taken as a condition of living-with God positively, then the two senses of orthodoxy blend into one.

It is also obvious that judgments of heresy presuppose a commitment to a prior orthodoxy. Given the fact that the substance of Christian life consists in three essentially distinct if interconnected ways of relating to things, it is possible to ask whether one or the other of these relations is more fundamental and so to that extent more determinative of orthodoxy. Is it more important for Christian life-with God that persons believe-that certain things are true? Is the boundary marker between orthodox and heretic a particular set of beliefs-that? This is evidently the historically more predominant attitude. But one might also wonder whether it is rather more essential that a person believe-in Jesus somewhat separately from his or her beliefs-that this or that might be true. Such an opinion can appear attractive especially in light of the difficulty with which disputes about differences of belief-that are resolved. The difficulty or even impossibility of definitively establishing some point of belief-that might inspire skepticism about the practice of anathematization and the contempt with which heretics are spoken about. Indeed, if one cannot be certain of the truth of one's beliefs-that, it would become all the more significant if one were to believe-in Jesus in spite of or perhaps even because of that fact. This is a question of considerable import that is taken up in greater detail in Section 5. It suffices for now simply to raise it as a possible line of inquiry.

1.3 The Question of Truth

Before proceeding to more concrete historical and theological matters in the subsequent sections, it would be well to pose a final question regarding the formal analysis of the concepts of orthodoxy and heresy. It has already been said that *orthodoxia* as *doxa* that is *orthē* is a matter of proper opinion or worship of God. But to what extent is *orthodoxia* a matter of truth?

Aristotle provides a very compelling definition of truth. "To say of what is that it is not, or of what is not that it is, is false, whereas to say of what is that it is, or of what is not that it is not, is true" (*Metaphysics* 1011b25). This definition seems acceptable and is taken for granted in the following. Truth is the relation of adequacy that obtains between what is said about something, on one hand, and the thing about which something is said, on the other. Truth is achieved when what is said is adequate to what is being talked about.

An honest person who believes-that this or that is the case generally has an interest in possessing the truth. This means that such a person has an interest in determining whether his or her beliefs-that are in fact true to the things themselves about which he or she believes them. But the determination of the truth of a proposition is not a matter of feeling one way or another about it. A proposition is not true (or false) simply because one is very strongly inclined to (dis)believe it. The possession of the truth is not signaled by a "monadic" state of spirit like feeling hungry or being sad would be. Truth is rather a relation, and the perception of a relation arguably requires the equal experiential givenness of the two related terms (Nemes 2019). If, then, truth is the relation of adequacy between what is said about something and that thing itself about which something was said, the "perception of truth" is only possible in the concrete experience of the thing itself about which one has some belief-that (Heidegger 1985: 51). One would see that the thing itself is such as one believes-that it is. For example, one sees the truth of one's belief-that there is someone in the home when one descends the stairs and finds a person in the hallway. The question of truth thus also brings with it a concern for the "perception of the truth."

To what extent is the truth so defined a criterion of Christian orthodoxy? To what extent are Christian faith and life a matter of "perceiving the truth" so understood? Here it is clearly a question of *orthē doxa* understood as proper or correct belief-that. Truth is a matter of saying of what is that it is and of what is not that it is not. Saying something about something is a matter of relating propositionally to that thing. Christians believe-that various things are the case – for example, that God exists and that Jesus was raised from the dead. But why do they believe-that as they do? What are the sources of Christian belief-that? To what extent is their believing-that a matter of seeing-that something is the case? And to what extent are the things about which Christians possess a diversity of beliefs-that themselves accessible to every person who believes about them in a Christian way?

These questions regarding the place of truth in the discussion about orthodoxy and heresy in Christian theology are significant. They are questions about the sources of Christian belief-that, but also questions about the nature of the things themselves to which Christian beliefs-that refer, specifically whether these are experientially accessible to Christians. These inquiries cannot be answered now but take center stage in Section 5.

2 Orthodoxy and Heresy in Christian Scripture

Scripture here refers to those uniquely authoritative biblical texts that together as the Old and New Testaments form a shared canon among Christians of the various confessional and ecclesial communities constituting Protestantism, Roman Catholicism, and Eastern Orthodoxy. There is no formal or philosophical discussion of the notions of orthodoxy and heresy as such in these texts, but they do propose a particular vision of what constitutes proper and improper ways of believing-that, believing-in, and living-with God and others in the community of the people of God. It is naturally impossible to be comprehensive given the limitations of the present context. This section limits itself to a discussion of the following *loci*: God the Creator in relation to the world and the human being, the revelation given at Sinai, the problem of idolatry, and Jesus and the apostles.

2.1 God, the World, and the Human Being

The Bible opens with a statement of the creation of the world by God. The Hebrew text of Gen. 1:1 reads: *bereishit bara' Elohim eit hashamayim v'eit ha'aretz*. According to the English translators of the New Revised Standard Version, this can be rendered in at least these three ways: "In the beginning when God created the heavens and the earth"; "When God began to create the heavens and the earth"; or "In the beginning God created the heavens and the earth." These differences of translation may be important for considering whether the Genesis text in particular teaches the doctrine of *creatio ex nihilo*. Admittedly, the idea that God creates things out of nothing does seem to appear in the New Testament. Paul speaks of "God . . . who gives life to the dead and calls into existence the things that do not exist" (Rom. 4:17). But this idea is arguably not present in the Genesis text (Levenson 1994: 5). In any case, the more important teaching of the Genesis text is that the world – together with everything that lives within it, including the human being – is the creation of the God of the Hebrew people.

If the world and the things of the world are the creation of God, then the question naturally arises whether God Himself has a creator. Jon Levenson very insightfully notes that "the God of Israel has no myth of origin. Not a trace of theogony can be found in the Hebrew bible" (Levenson 1994: 5). This point is highly significant for the Hebrew understanding of God. Indeed, on this point Genesis can be fruitfully compared with the creation mythologies of other societies of the ancient Near East. In the *Enuma Elish* or *The Epic of Creation* (Dalley 2009: 233–277), the order of the world comes about via warfare between gods who arose out of a mixture of Apsu and Tiamat, "the subterranean fresh waters ... and the saline waters of the oceans" (Levenson 1994: 3–4). Marduk, the son of the god Ea, defeats Tiamat and forms the world out of her mangled body (Dalley 2009: 254–255). Genesis presents things very differently. The God who creates the world does not come from anyone else, nor must He first conquer a hostile enemy in battle in order to create something new from the entrails of His victim. He simply speaks and things appear in obedience to His will (Gen. 1:3, 6, 9, 11, 14–15, 20, 24, 26). Levenson thus writes:

> We can capture the essence of the idea of creation in the Hebrew Bible with the word "mastery." The creation narratives, whatever their length, form, or context, are best seen as dramatic visualizations of the uncompromised mastery of YHWH, God of Israel, over all else. He alone is "the Lord of all the earth," and when the cosmogonic events are complete, his lordship stands beyond all doubt. (Levenson 1994: 3)

One could say that God has mastery over all things because He alone exists of Himself and nothing else exists apart from Him. The doctrines of creation and of providence are thus closely related in the understanding of God presented in the Bible.

The Hebrew Bible is notable not only for its depiction of God but also for the way it presents human beings. One important aspect of Genesis is its presentation of the creation of the human being as peaceful. On the sixth day of creation, God said, "Let us make humankind [*adam*] in our image, according to our likeness; and let them have dominion over the fish of the sea, and over the birds of the air, and over the cattle, and over all the wild animals of the earth, and over every creeping thing that creeps upon the earth" (Gen. 1:26). The human being is formed "from the dust of the ground" and is made to live when God "breathe[s] into his nostrils the breath of life" (Gen. 2:7). Genesis thus contrasts starkly with the creation of the human being as told in the Babylonian *Atrahasis* myth. This teaches that there was once a labor dispute between classes of divinities.

"When the gods instead of man did the work, bore the loads, the gods' load was too great, the work was too hard, the trouble too much, the great Annunaki made the Igigi carry the workload sevenfold" (Dalley 2009: 9). The toil of caring for the earth was too great and the Igigi rebelled. This rebellion awoke the Annunaki from their rest. The response to the problem was to create the human being. "Belet-ili the womb-goddess is present – Let her create primeval man so that he may bear the yoke ... Let man bear the load of the gods!" (Dalley 2009: 14). And so Ilawela, "who had intelligence," was slaughtered and the human being was created from his flesh and blood mixed with clay (Dalley 2009: 15–16). The *Atrahasis* myth thus sees the creation of the human being as having its origin in and taking place through violence and struggle, whereas Genesis sees the creation of the human being as a further instance of the omnipotent mastery of the Creator over a peaceful and reconciled created order (cf. Nemes 2016: 71–72).

The human being is also said to have been created "in the image and likeness of God" (Gen. 1:26–27). The theological interpretation of this phrase in the greater context of Christian thought is a matter of controversy. After comparing Genesis with other ancient Near Eastern sources, J. Richard Middleton comes to the conclusion that

> the description of ancient Near Eastern kings as the image of god ... provides the most plausible set of parallels for interpreting the *imago Dei* in Genesis 1. If such texts – or the ideology behind them – influenced the biblical *imago Dei*, this suggests that humanity is dignified with a status and role vis-à-vis the nonhuman creation that is analogous to the status and role of kings in the ancient Near East vis-à-vis their subjects ... As *imago Dei*, then, humanity in Genesis 1 is called to be the representative and intermediary of God's power and blessing on earth. (2005: 121)

Each human being would be the image of God in the sense that he or she has the calling of mediating the authority and benevolence of God to the world.

One point of agreement between Genesis and the ancient Near Eastern mythologies considered thus far is that the human being was tasked by God with working the earth: "God blessed them, and God said to them, 'Be fruitful and multiply, and fill the earth and subdue it; and have dominion over the fish of the sea and over the birds of the air and over every living thing that moves upon the earth'" (Gen. 1:28). But even in this agreement there is a greater and more significant disagreement. Unlike the *Enuma Elish* and *Atrahasis* myths, Genesis does not teach that human beings were created so as to free God from tiresome labor that no one else was around to do. To the contrary, they are sooner seen as coworkers of God and collaborators in the project of caring for the created order. Neither does God create man only to later retreat into His own domain. Rather, there is reference in Gen. 3:8 to "the sound of the lord God walking in the garden at the time of the evening breeze." This is a very strange notion for those who are accustomed to think of God as an all-powerful spirit. Whatever the metaphysical interpretation of the "walking," the image itself is highly suggestive: God does not intend to live apart from human beings but rather wants them to be in His company. He creates them so as to live-with them.

The biblical conception of God in relation to the world and the human being can be summarized as follows. God is the creator of them both. He is the creator and Lord of all things because nothing exists apart from His will, whereas He exists on His own and owes His reality to no one else. God created human beings in His image so as to live-with them as His collaborators in the project of caring for the created world.

2.2 Revelation at Sinai

Upon their creation, human beings sin and are cast out of God's presence (Gen. 3). Yet God does not abandon His purpose of living-with human beings. The principal concern of the Old Testament is the history of the people of Israel as the chosen people of God. It begins with the calling of Abram out of Ur of the Chaldees (Gen. 12). God promises Abram that He will make a great nation of out of him and that He will give to Abram and his offspring the land of Canaan (Gen. 17). Changing Abram's name to Abraham, God establishes circumcision as the sign of the covenant formed with Him. And yet, before the inheritance of the promised land can take place, his descendants must be slaves in a foreign land for four hundred years (Gen. 15:13–14). This is the slavery in Egypt from which the Hebrews were liberated in the Exodus through Moses (Exod. 1–15). After a number of plagues and trials and misfires along the way, they are led out of Egypt to Mt. Sinai, where God speaks to Moses and forms a covenant with the people (Exod. 19–24). This covenant includes laws (*torah*) that the people are to obey and that are to structure their society as God's people. These laws are then read a second time just before the people of Israel enter Canaan from the east in order to conquer it (Deut. 5ff.).

If the human being collaborates with God in caring for the world, the question can also be raised whether the human being collaborates with God in the process of revelation. How much of the Bible is from God and how much of it is human tradition? Sommer (2015: ch. 2) distinguishes between "minimalist" and "maximalist" approaches to the matter of exactly how much revelational content the people of Israel witnessed and received from God at Mt. Sinai in Exod. 19–24. Exod. 19 describes the event as characterized by "thunder and lightning, as well as a thick cloud on the mountain, and a blast of a trumpet so loud that all the people who were in the camp trembled" (Exod. 19:16). What is going on here? The minimalist tradition emphasizes that divine revelation is minimal in antecedently intelligible content, so it must be complemented by human interpretation. As Abraham Joshua Heschel writes: "Judaism is based upon a minimum of revelation and a maximum of interpretation, upon the will of God and upon the understanding of Israel" (1955: 274). And elsewhere he contends: "As a report about revelation the Bible itself is a *midrash*" (185). Sommer believes that the hermeneutical difficulties of Exod. 19 – "full of ambiguities, gaps, strange repetitions, and apparent contradictions" – demonstrate that "the extraordinary event chapter 19 describes was witnessed through a fog, or that the narrative of that event could not be articulated in human words; further, one senses that the text combines multiple recollections of an essentially unreportable event" (Sommer 2015: 32–33). Thus, for Sommer the Torah was not dictated or entirely inspired by God but is rather "a [human interpretive] response to God's act of revelation" (29). Incidentally, this is a relief for him insofar as it allows one to dissociate God from the morally problematic aspects of the Bible (27–28).

Connected to the giving of the Law is what would later be called rabbinic Judaism (cf. Berger 1998: ch. 2). At the second telling of the Law before the entry into Canaan, Moses leaves the following command:

> If a judicial decision is too difficult for you to make between one kind of bloodshed and another, one kind of legal right and another, or one kind of assault and another – any such matters of dispute in your towns – then you shall immediately go up to the place that the lord your God will choose, where you shall consult with the levitical priests and the judge who is in office in those days; they shall announce to you the decision in the case. Carry out exactly the decision that they announce to you from the place that the lord will choose, diligently observing everything they instruct you. You must carry out fully the law that they interpret for you or the ruling that they announce to you; do not turn aside from the decision that they announce to you, either to the right or to the left. As for anyone who presumes to disobey the priest appointed to minister there to the lord your God, or the judge, that person shall die. So you shall purge the evil from Israel. All the people will hear and be afraid, and will not act presumptuously again. (Deut. 17:8–13)

It may seem that the passage has in mind something else altogether than the rabbinic project. It speaks of what to do when a case presents itself that is "too difficult" for lower courts and seems to have to do only with matters of civil and criminal law. Even so, Michael Berger argues, the critical terms of this verse ("the judge," "a judicial decision," "any such matters of dispute") can be taken as sufficiently ambiguous to permit their being understood with respect to the project of legal interpretation of the Talmudic rabbis of later generations (1998: 32–37). The Sages and later the rabbis become "the judge who is in office in those days." These exercise their authority to "bind and loose" – that is, to forbid or permit certain practices or opinions, as well as to include or exclude persons from the community of God's people (Singer 1906: 215; cf. Josephus 1998: 1.5.2). And to the extent that the independently intelligible content of divine revelation is minimal, the word of the authorized interpreters of that revelation becomes all the more authoritative on its own.

Hyam Maccoby writes that the Pharisees of New Testament times and just before were the progenitors of the rabbis of rabbinic Judaism from after the destruction of the Temple in 70 CE (1988: 9–16). These were principally concerned with the propagation and interpretation of the so-called Oral Torah, "a living, growing body of law and lore, responding to changing circumstances and becoming more comprehensive in scope as the unfolding of time posed new questions" (4). At the same time, this Oral Torah is fallible. "There is ... in rabbinic Judaism nothing corresponding to the Catholic doctrine of the 'infallibility of the Church'" (4–5). This fallibility is illustrated by the story of the excommunication of Rabbi Eliezer in the Babylonian Talmud *Bava Metzia* 59b. Although Eliezer can respond to every objection offered against an opinion of his, although miracles are performed to confirm his point of view, and although a voice from heaven expresses agreement with his view as opposed to that of his opponents, nevertheless he is excommunicated on the basis of majority rule: "After a majority to incline" (Exod. 23:2). Rabbi Yehoshua even responds to the voice from heaven as follows: "It is not in heaven" (Deut. 30:12). *Bava Metzia* 59b explains the meaning of this: "Since the Torah was already given at Mount Sinai, we do not regard a Divine Voice, as You already wrote at Mount Sinai, in the Torah: 'After a majority to incline' (Exodus 23:2). Since the majority of Rabbis disagreed with Rabbi Eliezer's opinion, the halakha is not ruled in accordance with his opinion." In fact, the passage in question does not support that reading. It says: "You shall not follow a majority in wrongdoing; when you bear witness in a lawsuit, you shall not side with the majority so as to pervert justice" (Exod. 23:2). But the belief was that "God, having given the right of decision by majority vote, could not intervene to influence the discussions of the rabbis" (Maccoby 1988: 5). And the Talmud reports that, in response to Rabbi Yehoshua's remark, God laughed and said: "My children have triumphed over me." Maccoby thus comments: "This daring story declares the right of those who shape the Oral Torah to make mistakes. The human process of reaching truth, or provisional truth, by an effort of reasoning and discussion is thus sanctified" (5).

In fact, there is an entire tractate (*Mishnah Horayot*) dedicated to the question of what to do in cases in which the Sanhedrin or high court of the rabbis makes erroneous judgments (Berger 1998: 64). But Berger notes that the interpretation of rabbinic "error" depends upon whether one adopts a maximalist or minimalist conception of the revelation given at Sinai. According to the maximalist perspective, the rabbis in principle do nothing other than pass down oral traditions that were given at Sinai without having been written down. Because there is an antecedent revelation that the rabbis were charged with transmitting to others, there is in principle the possibility of an error in transmission, although the actuality of such an error remains impossible to determine because there is no access to that prior revelation apart from what the Sages passed down (Berger 1998: 65). On the other hand, if one opts for a minimalist perspective according to which the rabbis merely were given rules for determining cases, then they are not so much capable of "error" understood as "falsehood," but rather merely of the appropriate or inappropriate implementation of these rules (66–67). In the latter case, the rabbis would not be so much "infallible" as "final" in the sense that there is no greater court of appeal beyond them (64).

According to these authors, then, the giving of the Law at Sinai is an event that involves both divine revelation and human interpretation. The more minimal the intelligible content of the former, the greater the necessity and authority for the community of the latter. The authority of the interpreters of the Law would appear to be more a matter of "finality" than anything else. The notion that in addition to being final they are also protected from genuine error by divine guidance is a faith commitment that cannot be proven (Berger 1998: ch. 6). They can be seen rather as collaborators with God in the project of caring for the world and for Israel, His people who are endowed with the significant responsibility and authority to determine things for themselves. If one can speak of "orthodoxy" and "heresy" in this context, these terms would have to be understood in a rather "positivist" fashion. Shmuel Goldin expresses the point well: "Truth is no longer defined as objective fact, but, rather, by loyalty to the process" for decision-making (Goldin 2008: 157). The authorized interpreters of the community come to decisions by following a process, and, if this process is obeyed, their conclusions must be accepted simply as such.

2.3 The Problem of Idolatry

God promised Abraham that He would be the god of his offspring (Gen. 17:8). Of all the commandments given to the people of Israel upon their exodus from Egypt, the most significant for understanding the subsequent history of the Jewish people is perhaps the "first and greatest":

> I am the lord your God, who brought you out of the land of Egypt, out of the
> house of slavery; you shall have no other gods before me. You shall not make
> for yourself an idol, whether in the form of anything that is in heaven above,
> or that is on the earth beneath, or that is in the water under the earth. You shall
> not bow down to them or worship them; for I the lord your God am a jealous
> God. (Exod. 20:2–5)

One could say that God establishes unique fidelity to Him as a condition of His
living-with the people.

And yet this condition is tested even before the people of Israel reach the
promised land of Canaan, when they create a golden calf and bow down to it
while Moses is still on Mt. Sinai receiving teaching from God (Exod. 32:1–10).
It is only upon the intercession of Moses that God does not entirely abandon the
Hebrews after their idol worship (Exod. 32:11–14, 30–35; 33:12–23). Upon
their entry into Canaan, a continual struggle takes place between the people of
Israel and God. The former persistently fall into idolatrous practices and fail to
follow the commandments of God's Law. Although God sends them messengers and prophets to call them to repentance, at some point His patience runs out
and they are taken away into exile, the northern kingdom of Israel to Assyria and
the southern kingdom of Judah to Babylon after the destruction of the temple
built by Solomon (2 Kings 17:5–18; 2 Chr. 5:25–26, 36:15–21). This occurred
in fulfillment of various curses laid down by God in the second telling of the
Law that should come upon the people if they do not obey His commandments
and live-with Him and each other as He required (Deut. 28:15–68).

At the same time, during the Babylonian exile, prophets speak about the
promise of God to be merciful once more to His people: "Comfort, O comfort
my people, says your God. Speak tenderly to Jerusalem, and cry to her that she
has served her term, that her penalty is paid, that she has received from the
Lord's hand double for all her sins" (Isa. 40:1–2). They assert the power of God
in doing so because He is the one who has created the world and keeps it in
being:

> Why do you say, O Jacob, and speak, O Israel, 'My way is hidden from the
> Lord, and my right is disregarded by my God'? Have you not known? Have
> you not heard? The Lord is the everlasting God, the Creator of the ends of the
> earth. He does not faint or grow weary; His understanding is unsearchable. He
> gives power to the faint, and strengthens the powerless. Even youths will faint
> and be weary, and the young will fall exhausted; but those who wait for the
> Lord shall renew their strength, they shall mount up with wings like eagles,
> they shall run and not be weary, they shall walk and not faint. (Isa. 40:27–31)

Here is what would become essential Jewish (and Christian) orthodoxy: the God
of Israel is the Creator of the world. Because He is the source of everything,

He is not limited in power. He controls all things, not only bringing the foreign kingdoms against Israel for their punishment but also saving them now from the hands of their enemies (Isa. 41:2–3, 8–10). In this way, God also distinguishes Himself from the idols of the peoples whose gods are fashioned out of created materials, who cannot see or hear or speak, and who have no control over things (Isa. 44:9–20). Because God is the creator of everything, "An image cannot represent who he is" (Goldingay 2014: 62). It is consequently the power of God as the creator and source of reality that provides hope for the people of Israel:

> Thus says the lord, your Redeemer, who formed you in the womb: I am the lord, who made all things, who alone stretched out the heavens, who by myself spread out the earth; who frustrates the omens of liars, and makes fools of diviners; who turns back the wise, and makes their knowledge foolish; who confirms the word of his servant, and fulfills the prediction of his messengers; who says of Jerusalem, "It shall be inhabited," and of the cities of Judah, "They shall be rebuilt, and I will raise up their ruins," who says to the deep, "Be dry – I will dry up your rivers"; who says of Cyrus, "He is my shepherd, and he shall carry out all my purpose"; and who says of Jerusalem, "It shall be rebuilt," and of the temple, "Your foundation shall be laid." (Isa. 44:24–28)

Therefore, it is with the return of the people from exile by the intervention of their God that their conviction of God's omnipotence and His providential control over all things is solidified and clarified. The announcement of Cyrus of Persia's conquering on Babylon and the return of the people of Israel to their land through the prophets of the lord (Yahweh) call to light the fact that "Yahweh's capacity to declare what is going to happen stems from and evidences the fact that Yahweh is the one who determines what is going to happen" (Goldingay 2014: 63–64). In this way too the Israelites' opposition to idol worship is also confirmed, insofar as it does not again become a central problem of the Jewish people's life-with God as recounted in the biblical narrative. "It can be said that Isaiah 40–55 offers the clearest articulation of monotheism in the Old Testament" (Goldingay 2014: 63).

2.4 Jesus Christ and His Apostles

The central figure of the New Testament is Jesus of Nazareth. The New Testament is principally concerned with retelling His teachings; announcing His death, resurrection, and ascension into heaven for all people to believe-in Him; and providing guidance and instruction for coordinating Christian belief-that and living-with in the context of the church. The essential content of early Christian preaching about Jesus is summarized by the words spoken by Peter in the house of the Gentile Cornelius:

> You know the message [God] sent to the people of Israel, preaching peace by Jesus Christ – he is Lord of all. That message spread throughout Judea, beginning in Galilee after the baptism that John announced: how God anointed Jesus of Nazareth with the Holy Spirit and with power; how he went about doing good and healing all who were oppressed by the devil, for God was with him. We are witnesses to all that he did both in Judea and in Jerusalem. They put him to death by hanging him on a tree; but God raised him on the third day and allowed him to appear, not to all the people but to us who were chosen by God as witnesses, and who ate and drank with him after he rose from the dead. He commanded us to preach to the people and to testify that he is the one ordained by God as judge of the living and the dead. All the prophets testify about him that everyone who believes in him receives forgiveness of sins through his name. (Acts 10:36–43)

Here are contained the essential contours of the testimony of the New Testament: the preaching and earthly ministry of Jesus through the power of the Holy Spirit, beginning with His baptism by John in the Jordan; His death by crucifixion; His resurrection and appearance to His disciples; and the subsequent commission of His followers to call all people to believe-in Him in light of His God-appointed role as the judge of all at the end of history.

The personal identity of Jesus is an important question for the New Testament (and for later orthodoxy). Following a distinction elucidated by Joseph Ratzinger (2004: 160ff.), one could say that Jesus is both "the Son of God" and "the Son." These two phrases do not mean the same thing. For example, Jesus asks His disciples: "Who do you say that I am?" Simon Peter responds: "You are the Messiah [*ho christos*], the Son of the living God" (Matt. 16:15–16). By calling Jesus "Messiah" and "Son of the living God," Peter means to refer to Him as the promised king of Israel and inheritor of the throne of King David, whose kingdom was promised to last forever (2 Sam. 7:12–17). In the Old Testament, the king of Israel is referred to as God's son by election: "You are my son, today I have begotten you" (Ps. 2:7). In the same way, the people of Israel as a whole are called God's son: "When Israel was a child, I loved him, and out of Egypt I called my son" (Hos. 11:1). To call Jesus the "Son of God" is therefore to refer to His election as the king of Israel and as the representative of the people as a whole.

But there is also a more profound sense in which Jesus is uniquely "the Son." The relation between Jesus as Son and God as Father is intimate to the extent that one can speak of it as ontological, as a union of being. Jesus says: "All things have been handed over to me by my Father; and no one knows the Son except the Father, and no one knows the Father except the Son and anyone to whom the Son chooses to reveal him" (Matt. 11:27). Thomas F. Torrance comments:

> Careful examination disclosed that the mutual relation of knowing between the Father and the Son . . . involved a mutual relation of *being* between them as well, and not only between the eternal Son and the Father but between the incarnate Son and the Father. This implies that we are given access to the closed circle of divine knowing between the Father and the Son only through cognitive union with Christ, that it is only through an interrelation of knowing and being between us and the incarnate Son, although in our case this union is one of participation through grace and not one of nature. (Torrance 1991: 58–59)

Torrance here highlights that the union between Father and Son is onto-epistemological apart from the Son's coming into the world. This means that Christ preexisted His coming into the world (cf. John 6:32–51; Phil. 2:5–11). And this intimate bond of an onto-epistemological nature is related succinctly in the Gospel according to John: "In the beginning was the Word, and the Word was with God, and the Word was God . . . And the Word became flesh and lived among us, and we have seen His glory, the glory as of a father's only son . . . No one has ever seen God. It is God the only Son, who is close to the Father's heart, who has made Him known" (John 1:1, 14, 18).

Because of the close connection between Christ and the Father, there would appear to be no having one without the other: "No one who denies the Son has the Father; everyone who confesses the Son has the Father also" (1 John 2:23). The apostles Peter and John preach: "There is salvation in no one else, for there is no other name under heaven given among mortals by which we must be saved" (Acts 4:12). This idea comes from the teaching of Jesus Himself: "I am the way, and the truth, and the life. No one comes to the Father except through me. If you know me, you will know my Father also" (John 14:6–7). Jesus puts Himself between God and all other human beings in a way that scandalizes, as when He interprets the Law of God with an authority and audacity not had by other scribes in the eyes of the masses (Matt. 7:28–29). The relation to God can take place only through Jesus.

The person of Jesus is therefore significant not only for the people of Israel as the promised inheritor of the throne of David, but also for all of humanity as Him by whom God created the world. "All things came into being through Him" (John 1:3), and "All things have been created through Him and for Him" (Col. 1:16). This latter verse would thus subordinate Jesus's election as the king of Israel and inheritor of the nations (cf. Ps. 2:7–8) to His status as Him by whom all things were created. When the Word comes into the world, He comes to inherit what is His own (cf. John 1:10–11). But beyond this, Jesus is also presented as savior. Joseph is told by an angel after he learns that Mary is pregnant apart from him: "Joseph, son of David, do not be afraid to take Mary as your wife, for the child conceived in her is from the Holy Spirit. She will bear a son, and you are to name him Jesus, for he will save his people from their sins" (Matt. 1:20–21). The name Jesus or Yehoshua/Yeshua was commonly understood to mean "Yahweh saves" (Turner 2008: 67). Thus, the very name of Jesus connects His identity with salvation. Indeed, in the Johannine literature, He is even called "the Savior of the world" (John 4:42; 1 John 4:14).

The salvation accomplished by Jesus takes place especially through His death and resurrection. His death is described as a ransom for all humanity (1 Tim. 2:4–6) and an atonement for the sins of the whole world (1 John 2:2). The apostle Paul explains that by dying by crucifixion, a death described as cursed in the Law of Moses, Jesus redeems those cursed by the Law because of their disobedience to it and gives them instead the promised gift of the Holy Spirit (Gal. 3:10–14). Although He is righteous and without sin (Heb. 4:15), in His death Jesus takes upon Himself everything that stands against sinful human beings in order that it not fall upon them, which Paul describes elsewhere as follows: "For our sake [God] made Him to be sin who knew no sin, so that in Him we might become the righteousness of God" (2 Cor. 5:21). In the same way, the resurrection of Christ is the guarantee of the resurrection of His followers and of all humanity (1 Cor. 15:20–22). One could say that death itself as the cessation of the possibility of human life-with God is the enemy to be defeated by Christ's own death and resurrection from the dead (1 Cor. 15:26). And because Jesus's death and resurrection are the means by which salvation is accomplished, the opinion that Christ did not come "in the flesh" and so did not really die is condemned as not coming from God (1 John 4:1–3), as is the opinion that there is no resurrection from the dead (1 Cor. 15:12–34). God's victory over death in Jesus is thus essential to the apostolic teaching.

Jesus famously chose twelve from among His disciples whom He called "apostles" because He sent them out to preach His message of the arrival of the kingdom of God (Matt. 10:1–7; Mark 3:13–14). These figures played an especially significant role in the development of the community of Jesus's followers after His resurrection and ascension into heaven. The earliest converts to the message of Christianity on the day of Pentecost were said to have "devoted themselves to the apostles' teaching and fellowship" (Acts 2:42). The apostle Paul later describes the church as the community of Jesus as built upon "the foundation of the apostles and the prophets, with Christ Jesus Himself as the cornerstone" (Eph. 2:20). At the same time, Paul describes the apostles and other messengers of the word about Christ elsewhere as "servants of Christ and stewards of God's mysteries" (1 Cor. 4:1). This implies that the authority of the apostles is ministerial rather than magisterial. They bear witness to Jesus's teachings.

Upon his confession of faith, Jesus endowed Peter with the "keys of the kingdom of heaven" (cf. Isa. 22:15–23) and promised him: "Whatever you bind on earth will have been bound in heaven, and whatever you loose on earth will have been loosed in heaven" (Matt. 16:19). This reference to "binding" and "loosing" hearkens back to the authority the Pharisees presumed for themselves as the authoritative interpreters of the Law for the people of Israel (Singer 1906: 215; Mansoor 2007: 31). At the same time, Jesus regularly disregarded and disobeyed the teaching and authority of the Pharisees (Mark 2:15–17, 2:23–28, 3:1–6, 7:1–8), complaining that they preferred human traditions to the commandment of God (Mark 7:6–13). He calls them "blind guides of the blind" and a "plant that my heavenly Father has not planted" (Matt. 15:13–14). The use of the perfect passive periphrastic – "will have been bound/loosed" – thus should be understood as implying that Peter, in contradistinction to the scribes and Pharisees, will exercise his authority to bind or loose in a way that is manifestly guided by the prior determinations of God (Nemes 2021b: 40).

Whereas the Pharisees believed that God's "commandments were to be interpreted in conformity with the standard and interpretation of the rabbis of each generation, and to be made to harmonize with advanced ideas" (Mansoor 2007: 31), Jesus means to subordinate Peter and the apostles' teaching to the word of God such as He explained it to them (cf. Matt. 28:20). In the context of the church, He alone is teacher and all others are mere students (Matt. 23:8–10).

The apostles exercised their authority in the community in a notably empirical manner. After the suicide of Judas, Peter decides that someone should be elected to replace him as one of the twelve on the basis of what he took to be Old Testament prophecy in the Psalms (Acts 1:15–22). Matthias is chosen by a casting of lots, through which method the apostles prayed that God would make His preference clear to them (Acts 1:24–26). Peter and John refuse to submit to the command of the Council to stop preaching in the name of Jesus because they had seen Him raised from the dead and miracles performed through His name: "Whether it is right in God's sight to listen to you rather than to God, you must judge; for we cannot keep from speaking about what we have seen and heard" (Acts 4:19–20; cf. 5:29). Peter also receives a vision in which he is told not to call profane what God has made clean, after which he is sent by the Holy Spirit to preach in the house of a Gentile named Cornelius (Acts 10:1–23).

Although Peter considers it unlawful for a Jew to enter the house of a Gentile, he tells the people that he has learned from God not to call anyone profane or unclean, and upon preaching the Gospel to the household of Cornelius he and his partners with him see them receive the Holy Spirit (Acts 10:24–46). Upon seeing this, Peter exclaims: "Can anyone withhold the water for baptizing these people who have received the Holy Spirit just as we have?" (Acts 10:47). And when Peter is questioned by other Jewish Christians in Jerusalem for having visited a Gentile, he recounts the story, commenting: "If then God gave them the same gift that He gave us when we believed in the Lord Jesus Christ, who was I that I could hinder God?" (Acts 11:17).

This becomes the basis for the decision of "the apostles and the elders" in Jerusalem to admit Gentiles into the church without imposing upon them complete obedience to the Law of Moses (Acts 15:6–29). These examples illustrate the manner in which the "binding in heaven" of which Christ spoke precedes the "binding on earth," specifically by the former becoming manifest in the world prior to and as a guide for the latter (Nemes 2021b: 40).

The preaching and argumentation of the apostles is also in many cases empirical. The apostles preach the resurrection of Jesus from the dead because they saw Him (cf. 1 Cor. 15:3–11). First John summarizes the message of the apostolic college as follows:

> We declare to you what was from the beginning, what we have heard, what we have seen with our eyes, what we have looked at and touched with our hands, concerning the word of life – this life was revealed, and we have seen it and testify to it, and declare to you the eternal life that was with the Father and was revealed to us. (1:1–2)

The apostles thus preach things they have seen and heard and touched themselves, things apparent within the manifest world of experience. Peter also preaches the resurrection of Christ by noting that he and the other disciples ate and drank with Him (Acts 10:41; cf. Luke 24:36–43). In the same way, in response to the news that some Gentiles in the Galatian churches had taken up circumcision and obedience to the Law, Paul appeals to their experience: "The only thing I want to learn from you is this: Did you receive the Spirit by doing the works of the law or by believing what you heard? Are you so foolish? Having started with the Spirit, are you now ending with the flesh?" (Gal. 3:2–3). The argument is thus that if one has received the promised Holy Spirit apart from works of the Law, then it would be a backward movement to turn toward the Law as a source of righteousness. These cases can thus serve as examples of the ways in which the apostles argued from experience and the manifestation of God's will in the world in order to exercise their authority as leaders of the earliest Christian communities.

3 Orthodoxy and Heresy in Church History

The question of "orthodoxy" and "heresy" in the sense of proper and improper belief-that was an important one for the church from the very beginning. The purpose of this section is to provide a brief survey of some of the more significant developments of Christian theology in this respect, focusing especially on the first millennium or so of church history. The discussion addresses the question of the true shape of apostolic Christianity, the trinitarian debates of the fourth century, the question of the use of images in worship, and the problem of the Real Presence of Christ's body and blood in the Eucharist.

3.1 Apostolic Christianity

Among the important and hotly debated questions of the second and third centuries was that of the nature and shape of truly apostolic Christianity. It is taken for granted that Jesus had a school of disciples whom He specifically taught and sent into the world to propogate His teaching. There is also the apostle Paul, who had not followed Jesus during His earthly ministry but to whom Christ had appeared after His resurrection and ascension and whom He had appointed apostle to the nations (Acts 9:15–16; Gal. 2:7–8). These apostles of Jesus and their close associates were thus the principal sources for the teachings of Jesus from the earliest days. But the interpretation of their words and message was a matter of significant controversy.

Because of the concrete path that history actually took, it is difficult to present apostolic preaching and its historical context from any other perspective but that of the winning party in these disputes, namely what later came to be called the "catholic" or "orthodox" tradition (cf. Pelikan 1971). On the other hand, there are scholars who maintain that the traditions later deemed heretical could plausibly claim a connection to and foundation in apostolic preaching and teaching, especially that of Paul (Bauer 1971: ch. 10). Mark Edwards (2009) argues that certain fundamental modes of reasoning of later "orthodoxy" theology were themselves contested in the case of the "heretical" theologies rejected by earlier generations of the church. Even so, because the majority of Christian readers and authors in the present day are in some way or another associated with this "catholic" or "orthodox" tradition, it should suffice to take this point of view for granted while at the same time attempting to be fair to its opponents. It is also impossible briefly to summarize every point of controversy between the "catholics" and the so-called Gnostics who competed against them.

Edwards (2009) draws from Porphyry the definition of Gnosticism: "to hold that the demiurge of the visible cosmos is malign" (13). The present discussion focuses specifically on the relationship between God and the created world, since this was also the major theme of the scriptural survey of Section 2.1.

One of the principal theological enemies of the "catholic" tradition in the second century was Marcion of Sinope. The roughly contemporary catholic bishop-theologian Irenaeus of Lyons summarizes his teaching in *Against Heresies* 1.27. Marcion is claimed to have succeeded Cerdo, who took from Simon Magus (cf. Acts 8:9–25) and his followers the teaching that the Creator God of the Old Testament was not the same God as the Father of Jesus Christ (*AH* 1.27.1). Marcion develops this theology further, amending and correcting the works that would later constitute the "catholic" New Testament by removing any proposed connection between Christ and the Creator (1.27.2). He taught that salvation is only achievable for those who learn of his doctrine and that this salvation affects only the soul and not the earthly body (1.27.3). At the same time, Irenaeus admits that Marcion accepts the authority of the apostles of Jesus even while daring to correct their testimony on certain points. In this sense, Marcion is no different from other "heretics," such as the Valentinians, who likewise defended their theology on the basis of the scriptural texts accepted by the "catholics" (cf. 1.1–9). For this reason, Irenaeus makes a special point of refuting not only the Marcionite doctrine but also the doctrines of the other "heretical" groups from the scriptures themselves (1.27.4). And, as he says elsewhere, "proofs [of the things which are] contained in the Scriptures cannot be shown except from the Scriptures themselves" (3.12.9). Arguments about the teaching of Scripture are to be established by comparative hermeneutics.

Against these opinions, Irenaeus claims that the Church throughout the whole world has received a single faith from the apostles (1.10.1). This faith affirms the existence of one God, "the Father almighty," the Creator of the world and of all things. It also affirms there is "one Christ Jesus, the Son of God, who became incarnate for our salvation." It also teaches about

> the Holy Spirit, who proclaimed through the prophets the dispensations of God, and the advents, and the birth from a virgin, and the passion, and the resurrection from the dead, and the ascension into heaven in the flesh of the beloved Christ Jesus, our Lord, and His [future] manifestation from heaven in the glory of the Father "to gather up all things in one," and to raise up anew all the flesh of the whole human race.

This is the truly apostolic faith, contrary to the claims of the "heretics." And it is notable for the universal (or "catholic") and comprehensive vision it proposes. The Christian faith does not reject one aspect of reality out of preference for another, as Marcion's theology does. Rather, it brings into unity the human being in soul and body, the created world, the history of the Jewish people, the person of Jesus, God His Father, and the future of humanity.

In the second book of *Against Heresies*, Irenaeus offers a number of scriptural arguments in favor of his own doctrine as against that of the "heretics." Indeed, he thinks that "the entire Scriptures, the prophets, and the Gospels, can be clearly, unambiguously, and harmoniously understood by all, although all do not believe them" (2.27.2). They plainly do not teach what the "heretics" are proposing. But he also notes that the comparative-hermeneutical approach is not always convincing and that sometimes the "heretics" will appeal to secret oral traditions passed down by teachers apart from all texts (3.2.1).

For this reason, in the beginning of the third book Irenaeus makes appeals to those churches throughout the world that are famous for having been founded by the apostles, in which the apostles designated certain persons as successors to their "place of government" and in which it is possible to enumerate the subsequent succession of leaders whose teachings are well known (3.3.1). These same leaders are variously called by Irenaeus "presbyters" and "bishops" – that is, "elders" and "overseers" (3.2.2; 3.3.1; 4.26.2–5; 4.32.1). These terms for him apparently refer to the same group of persons, unlike in later history (see Stewart 2014; cf. Sullivan 2001; Lampe 2003). More to the point, the bishops or presbyters of the apostle-founded churches Irenaeus has in mind "neither taught nor knew of anything like what these [heretics] rave about" (3.3.1). Indeed, they were specially and carefully chosen by the apostles to lead the churches left by them precisely because if the wrong person were appointed to the position of elder or overseer, it would be "the direst calamity" for the church (3.3.1).

Because it would be "tedious" to enumerate the succession of teachers in all the apostle-founded churches, Irenaeus makes special appeal to "the very great, the very ancient, and universally known church founded and organized at Rome by the two most glorious apostles, Peter and Paul" (3.3.2). He says that "it is indeed a matter of necessity that every church agrees with this church, on account of its greater preeminence" (*ad hanc enim ecclesiam propter potiorem principalitatem necesse est omnem convenire ecclesiam*). But some scholars note that this should not be understood as though agreement with the theology of the Roman church were a matter of theological principle valid for all times and places (Eno 1990: 39; Osborn 2001: 129–130; cf. McGuckin 2008: 91). Rather, the necessity at stake is conditional in nature. He is saying in effect that, since all the other churches founded by apostles hold the Roman church in high esteem, they must also agree with its teaching and consider it genuinely apostolic in nature, and if the esteemed Roman church knows nothing of the teachings of the heretics, then this would suffice to prove that these teachings cannot be genuinely apostolic.

Some of the "heretics" did not have a problem arguing that even the apostles may have been mistaken or ignorant about this or that (*AH* 3.2.2). Against this, Irenaeus maintains that the Old Testament scriptures, if read "with attention," can be seen to have been fulfilled in what took place in Christ as reported in the

New Testament (4.26.1). The person and history of Christ is the interpretive key by which the salvific benefit of Scripture can be discovered and appreciated, just like a treasure hidden in a field (cf. Matt. 13:18). The apostles learned this key from Christ Himself and passed it down to the presbyters in the church (*AH* 4.26.1). Irenaeus on this basis proposes that "it is incumbent to obey the presbyters who are in the Church – those who . . . possess the succession from the apostles; those who, together with the succession of the episcopate, have received the certain gift of truth [*charisma veritatis certum*], according to the good pleasure of the Father" (4.26.2).

This "certain gift of truth" is interpreted by some to refer to a charism of infallibility and providential divine guidance belonging to the office of the bishop (cf. Kelly 1968: 37; Dulles 2017: 22–23). But this position apparently assumes that "bishop" and "presbyter" refer to distinct offices in Irenaeus, contrary to what was mentioned earlier. For example, Irenaeus says that there are presbyters "puffed up with the pride of holding the chief seat" (4.26.3). He could not describe the position of presbyter as "the chief seat" if, in his mind, the position of bishop were higher. Thus the "succession of the episcopate" (*episcopatus successione*) mentioned here does not refer to a distinct order from that of the presbyters, as though the presbyters had to be in submission to bishops (so Swinburne 2007: 183–184). It rather should be understood as the "succession to the episcopate." The episcopate is the office occupied by a presbyter. If the episcopate were not occupied by the presbyters, then Irenaeus's argument would be needlessly weak. He could have made a stronger argument by insisting on obedience to the bishops. This suggests that, for him, the episcopate is the office occupied by a presbyter.

Irenaeus admits that the first bishops had to be carefully chosen by the apostles lest they fall away and lead the churches into error (*AH* 3.3.1). He also admits that there are presbyters in the church who should not be followed precisely because they live in sin and do not keep the doctrine of the apostles (4.26.3–4). There would consequently seem to be nothing about the position of bishop/presbyter as such that involves or implies a special charism of infallibility. In speaking of the "certain gift of truth," he should rather be understood as referring to the apostolic hermeneutic by which the Scriptures are understood with reference to birth, life, death, and resurrection of Christ.

As Irenaeus says earlier: "It is not necessary to seek the truth among others which it is easy to obtain from the Church; since the apostles, like a rich man [depositing his money] in a bank, lodged in her hands most copiously all things pertaining to the truth: so that every man, whosoever will, can draw from her the water of life" (3.4.1). And as later: "True knowledge is [that which consists in] the doctrine of the apostles, and the ancient constitution of the Church throughout the whole world, and the distinctive manifestation of the body of Christ according to the succession of the bishops" (4.33.8).

Irenaeus therefore proposes two fundamental arguments against Marcion and the other "heretics." First, he argues at great length that the Scriptures cannot reasonably be interpreted as they propose. This is a comparative-hermeneutical argument. The "catholic" or "orthodox" interpretation is plainly more adequate to the texts than that of the "heretics." Anyone who reads the Scripture in the way of the apostolic churches can experience their salvific power. Second, he argues that the unanimity of teaching maintained by the succession of presbyters/bishops in the various churches that the apostles themselves founded throughout the world testifies to the truth of their claim to be of genuinely apostolic origin. This is more of an empirical and historical argument, the strength of which lies in the fact that he can appeal to persons whom he personally knew and who were in contact with the apostles themselves (cf. 3.3.4). Finally, it is possible to synthesize these two Irenaean arguments as follows. The apostolic interpretation of the Scriptures, as preserved and passed down in the various apostolic churches themselves, is plainly the superior interpretation insofar as its adequacy to the texts and salvific power can be appreciated by anyone.

3.2 The Father and the Son

Whereas the debate between Irenaeus and the Gnostics was a matter of disagreement between the "catholic" and "orthodox" traditions and those who did not accept the essential shape of the purportedly apostolic teaching, in the trinitarian controversies of the fourth century, one is confronted with a debate taking place within the interior of the apostolic and "catholic" tradition itself. This debate principally concerned the ontological question of the relation between Christ the Son and God the Father.

Jesus said: "The Father and I are one" (John 10:30). The question in the present context is whether this is a unity of being or a unity of will (Anatolios 2011: 30). Is the Son "of the same nature" (*homoousios*) as the Father? Are they one in being? If He is indeed of the same nature, this might imply that He was not "created" but is rather eternally "begotten." This latter term would then denote a unique asymmetrical relation of ontological dependence that does not imply standing on the other side of the divide between Creator and creature. Such was the opinion of Athanasius of Alexandria, then a deacon, who in this matter followed his bishop, Alexander. He wrote his famous work *Against the Gentiles / On the Incarnation* (1971) defending the view that Jesus is the incarnation of the Word of God, of one substance with the Father.

This proposal was made in conscious opposition to the opinion of a presbyter named Arius, who apparently maintained that the Son was only the first and most exalted creature of God, by whom all other things were created. Because the Father is "ontologically other than" (*heteroousios*) the Son, even the Son does not know or worship Him perfectly but only in part, as much and as well as is possible for a creature (Ayres 2004: 55). The Son is at most the highest and paradigmatic creature, an "exemplar" for the others through His submission to God and unity with Him in will (Anatolios 2011: 47). But statements of these sorts were considered highly impious and offensive to the ears of Athanasius and others like him.

A number of important figures became involved in this debate. Khaled Anatolios provides a helpful sketch of the contours of the debate and of the convictions of the principal *dramatis personae*. All the theologians were in agreement on the basic content of the apostolic teaching of Scripture, on the connection between the office of bishop and the authoritative interpretation of that teaching, and on the primacy of faith over reason as well as on the necessity of applying reason to faith (Anatolios 2011: 36). They also agreed that Father, Son, and Holy Spirit were the objects of Christian faith and worship, that God created the world from nothing, and that Christ is Lord in such a way as to rule out His being "merely" man (36–37). Among those who maintained an ontological distinction between Father and Son while emphasizing a unity of will (*symphonia*) were Arius, Asterius, Eusebius of Caesarea (at least in the beginning of the controversy), and Eunomius of Cyzicus (42–79). Among those who maintained a unity of being between Father and Son were Alexander of Alexandria, Marcellus of Ancyra, Apollinaris of Laodicea (79–97).

The drama of this controversy is long and complicated (see especially Behr 2001, 2004; Ayres 2004; Anatolios 2011). It will suffice for present purposes to note that a number of councils were held in this time, each supporting the opinion of a particular party within the greater context of the dispute. The most famous of these is the Council of Nicaea convened by the Roman emperor Constantine I in 325 CE. It consecrated the Athanasian position that the Son was "consubstantial" with the Father (*homoousios Patri*) by inserting this phrase into its famous creed.

After the creed came two anathemas against those who affirm that "there once was a time when the Son was not" and that the Son was "mutable or subject to change." The use of the word *homoousios* to describe the Son's relationship with the Father was controversial, since some understood it to suggest that the Father and Son shared a single material substratum (Ayres 2004: 93). The Nicene position, on the other hand, put it forth for the sake of an affirmation of fundamental ontological identity between Father and Son beyond all comparison with material realities. The council was also controverted because it was supported by Marcellus of Ancyra, suspected of being a Sabellian who held that the distinctions between Father, Son, and Holy Spirit were merely economic, having to do with the stages or manifestations of the providential work of God in history rather than being real distinctions (Ayres 2004: 62).

A number of bishops gathered in Antioch in 341 CE at the dedication of a church built by Emperor Constantius. They used the occasion to release a number of statements regarding the Arian controversy. The second text contains a statement of faith in which Father, Son, and Holy Spirit are described as three *hypostaseis* who are "one in agreement" (*symphonia*; Ayres 2004: 118). It deliberately avoids using the word *homoousios*. Lewis Ayres notes that Athanasius considered this creed Arian whereas Hilary of Poitiers thought it pro-Nicene (Ayres 2004: 121).

Two more councils gathered in the 350s as Constantius gained control over the entire empire. The first council at Sirmium in 351 CE was concerned to enforce the decision of earlier councils to depose Photinus, the bishop of Sirmium (Ayres 2004: 134). His principal accuser was Basil of Ancyra. This council issued a creed that was largely identical to the fourth creed issued earlier at Antioch as well as a series of anathemas condemning the use of *ousia* language to describe the relationship between Father and Son. The concern appears to have been that "linking the Son and Father with *ousia* language implies that the Father's being is 'extended' (*platunesthai*) in the generation of the Son" (134.) There were also attacks on the notion that "Father and Son are coeternal or two (equal) Gods" (134).

A confession of faith was also emitted by a later gathering of bishops at Sirmium in 357 CE that condemned the use of *ousia* language in describing the relationship between Father and Son altogether. "Strong ambivalence to Nicaea, or a wish to avoid its terms, has turned to direct opposition" (Ayres 2004: 138). From this text emerged the "Homoian" party, which sought "to find a solution to the ongoing controversy that would rule out any theologies seemingly tainted with Marcellan emphases" (138). This party preferred to say that the Son was "like" (*homoios*) the Father in all respects, without calling Him "consubstantial" (*homoousios*). In response to the development of a "Heterousian" wing within the "Homoian" party, another small council met in 358 CE in Ancyra at the invitation of Basil, its bishop. Here it was argued that the likeness in activity between Father and Son implies a likeness of essence and that the relationship between the two was unknowable except insofar as it is not like that between Creator and creature (149–151).

Constantius determined in 359 CE to call a general council as his father Constantine did in the manner of Nicaea (Ayres 2004: 157). In fact, two councils met: a western council at Arminium and an eastern council in Seleucia (160). The creed considered at these councils asserted that Father and Son are alike in all respects, as the Scriptures teach, but it condemned the use of *ousia* language "because it was inserted into the creed of Nicaea 'though not familiar to the masses,' because it caused 'disturbance,' and because it is unscriptural" (158). The majority of those gathered at the western council were willing to accept the creed with the exception of the phrase "in all things" used to qualify the likeness of the Son to the Father.

At least one factor involved in this agreement was deceit and coercion: Constantius had made clear he would exile anyone who did not agree to the creed, and he lied to the western bishops that the eastern council had already submitted to it (Ayres 2004: 161). Then, with similar difficulty and questionable maneuvering, agreement was reached about the creed at the eastern council in Seleucia. In 360 CE a council was held in Constantinople that emitted a "Homoian" creed that rejected all language of *ousia* to describe the relationship between Father and Son. This creed "remained the imperially sanctioned statement of orthodoxy for almost two decades (especially clearly in the east)" (165).

After the ascension to the throne on the part of Emperor Theodosius, the Nicene perspective was enforced in the city of Constantinople beginning in the year 380 CE. "Heretics" were forbidden to gather for worship, and those who did not confess to the trinitarian perspective of Nicaea were forced to abandon their churches to bishops who did (Ayres 2004: 253–254). Then a council was held in Constantinople in 381 CE that is believed to have emitted what today is known as the Nicene–Constantinopolitan Creed. The generally Nicene tenor of the theology of the council was a fait accompli from the beginning, and the council itself was probably not intended as "an 'ecumenical' reaffirmation of Nicaea" (255). Although this council represents for many the victory of Nicene "orthodoxy" over heresy, Ayres notes that Constantinople "does not mark the end of Trinitarian debate in the eastern empire," that "anti-'Arian' writings were produced into the 420s," and "many of the non-Nicene groups flourished beyond this date" (259–260).

Walter Bauer (1971) famously argued that the first forms of Christianity to appear in many areas of the ancient world were precisely such as would be condemned as heretical by later generations (see also Köstenberger and Kruger 2010; Hartog 2015). This is contrary to the more traditional opinion that "orthodoxy" always precedes "heresy" in time, so the orthodox faith is what was always believed from the beginning (cf. Tertullian, *Prescription against the Heretics* 29–31). And Edwards (2009) argues that the historical development and elucidation of "orthodoxy" in later generations drew from and was influenced by ideas deemed "heretical" by earlier ones. These theses can be appreciated in the context of the trinitarian controversy. The trinitarian dispute between the deacon Athanasius and the presbyter Arius brought to the fore the true diversity of opinion on the question within the interior of the "catholic" tradition.

Despite the fact that it is "heresy" for later generations, Arius's opinion was neither unthinkable nor totally alien to the understanding of bishops in various quarters of the "catholic" church in his own time. Ayres argues that the Arian controversy must be seen as "occurring with and because of tension between existing theological trajectories" at that time (2004: 84; emphasis removed). Vladimir Latinovic even makes the argument that Arius's opinion could have been considered quite a conservative one in certain places. This explains why it had sympathizers in so many quarters of the Christian world for so long: it resonated with their inherited conception of the faith. This also makes sense of why the Western bishops Palladius and Secundianus could defend themselves from the accusation of Arianism at the council of Aquileia (381 CE) by claiming that they did not know who Arius was, nor what he taught, nor what he looked like (Latinovic 2017: 33).

Thus, although there is no denying that Arius's opinion was taken for granted as "heretical" by the majority of Christians in the "catholic" tradition in the later history of the church, it is also apparent that many figures within the interior of the "catholic" tradition during his time and somewhat after did not share this point of view. And even among those who found his opinion disagreeable, there was no agreement as to what is proper – for example, the Homoians, Homoiousians, and Nicenes disagreed about the propriety of using *ousia* language.

The significance of this discussion can be appreciated as follows. With Marcion and the Gnostics, the "heresy" was a matter of seeing Jesus Christ and His Father as exclusive of and separable from the God of the Old Testament and the material world He had created. In the trinitarian controversies of the fourth century, on the other hand, the "heresy" was a matter of seeing God the Father as utterly distinct and theoretically separable from His Son. The Nicene affirmation of the consubstantiality (*homoousia*) of Father and Son implies that "No one who denies the Son has the Father; everyone who confesses the Son has the Father also" (1 John 2:23). There is no Father without a Son and no Son without a Father (cf. Torrance 1991, 2016). The two are inseparable as God: "So of necessity the Word is in his begetter and the begotten coexists eternally with the Father" (Athanasius, *Against the Gentiles* 47).

3.3 Images

Another controversy of significance for Christian theology and the problem of "orthodoxy" had to do with the use and veneration of images in Christian worship. At Exod. 20:4–5 the Hebrews received this commandment from God: "You shall not make for yourself an idol, whether in the form of anything that is in heaven above, or that is on the earth beneath, or that is in the water under the earth. You shall not bow down to them or worship them; for I the Lord your God am a jealous God, punishing children for the iniquity of parents, to the third and the fourth generation of those who reject me." The question was whether the veneration of images constituted a violation of the command to worship God alone.

Emperor Leo III interpreted hardships falling upon the Byzantine empire in the eighth century as divine punishment for breaking this commandment through the presence and veneration of icons. By way of response, in 730 CE he enacted an "iconoclastic" decree that called for the prohibition and destruction of religious images, inviting and later punishing the opposition of Popes Gregory II and III (Giakalis 2005: 7–8). His successor, Constantine V, later developed a dogmatic theology of iconoclasm and sought its ratification by means of an ecumenical council that gathered in Hiereia in 754 CE, although the pope and the Eastern patriarchs were not present (8–9). The *Definition* propagated by the council of Hiereia "censure[d] the honouring of icons as a practice leading to idolatry . . . on the grounds that it was opposed to Scripture and holy tradition and not authorized by the first ecumenical councils" (10). It also rejected the idea that Christ could be depicted as implying Nestorianism or Monophysitism: "Since the divinity and humanity have been united in Christ in one person without confusion or division, anyone who confesses Christ as a person depicted pictorially either takes him to be a mere man or confuses the two natures and presents the divine nature and the divine hypostasis as circumscribed" (10). It allowed only one icon of Christ, the one left by God – the bread of the Eucharist.

Constantine V was succeeded by his son Leo IV, who lessened the persecution of the iconophiles without definitively repealing the iconoclastic legislation. Then he died suddenly and was succeeded by his son, Constantine VI. But since he was only ten years old and too young to rule, Empress Irene assumed the regency (Giakalis 2005: 11–12). She arranged for the election of a new patriarch of Constantinople by popular vote in 784 CE: a layman Tarasius, who agreed to the election "on the condition . . . that an Ecumenical Council should be convened which would settle definitively the question of icons and would establish peace and unity in the Church and the empire" (13). This council was convened in Constantinople in 786 CE after having been preceded by a significant exchange of correspondence between Tarasius and other patriarchs, including Pope Adrian I, as well as between Adrian I and the imperial couple (13–15). This council was chaotically interrupted by "a large body of imperial guards loyal to the memory of Constantine V," so that the "first attempt at convening an Ecumenical Council thus ended in disorder, choked by violence and the clash of wild passions" (15–16).

Irene replaced the imperial guard with iconophile troops from Thrace and convened the council once more in Nicaea in 787 CE, beginning in September. Meeting in eight sessions, this council received bishops who wanted to convert from their iconoclastic error, refuting the argumentation of the iconoclastic Council of Hiereia (754 CE) and anathematizing those who participated in it and those who accepted its theology, including three leading iconoclasts and three iconoclast patriarchs. It also taught that "the cross and representations of Christ and the saints may be depicted on the walls of churches in order to stimulate the remembrance of the prototypes, and that these may be venerated with lights, incense and kissing, but not with the true worship (*latreia*) that belongs to God alone" (Giakalis 2005: 20). "The council of 787 was pronounced Ecumenical and was accepted as such in spite of the reservations of Rome and of the patriarchates of Alexandria, Antioch and Jerusalem on account of the way the latter were represented" (20–21). This council initially was not received well in the West. The Council of Frankfurt (794 CE) maintained that images were merely decorative and didactic in function, and a similar position was taken in 823 CE at the Council of Paris (21).

Both the iconoclasts and the iconophiles were concerned to argue for their perspectives from Scripture and the "catholic" tradition. Recalling here the traditional opinion of the priority of orthodoxy to heresy (cf. Tertullian, *Prescription against the Heretics* 29–31), it is noteworthy that both groups were concerned to argue for the novelty and innovation of the other position.

The iconoclasts tried to argue that refusal of image veneration is most consonant with Scripture and ancient Christian tradition. Leo III asked the pointed question: "Tell me, whoever taught us to venerate and revere images made by human hands?" (Giakalis 2005: 23). They appealed to the prohibition of image worship at Exod. 20:4, to King Hezekiah's removal of the bronze serpent from the temple after eight hundred years at 2 Kings 18:4, and to passages such as John 4:24, which states: "God is spirit and those who worship must worship in spirit and truth" (24). They also appealed to passages in Athanasius, Gregory of Nazianzus, Basil of Caesarea, John Chrysostom, Theodotus of Ancyra, and Amphilochius of Iconium, although, Ambrosios Giakalis comments, "Most of these witnesses seem colourless and irrelevant – detached phrases taken out of their original context" (25). He allows two considerable witnesses. The first is a fragment from a letter of Eusebius of Caesarea to Augusta Constantia, sister of Constantine I, in which the bishop argues that Christ in His glorified state cannot be depicted (25–26). The second is a passage from the *Testament* of Epiphanius of Salamis: "Keep it in mind not to set up icons in churches, or in the cemeteries of the saints, but always have God in your hearts through remembrance. Do not even have icons in private houses. For it is not permissible for the Christian to let his eyes wander or indulge in reveries" (quoted in Giakalis 2005: 26).

The iconophiles also argued from Scripture and from the witness of the Fathers. From the instruction to create golden cherubim for the mercy seat (Exod. 25:17–22) they drew the conclusion that "objects made by human hands do exist for the service and glory of God" (Giakalis 2005: 31). They also considered the creation and veneration of icons an unwritten apostolic tradition, evidence of which is the fact that these practices were found throughout the whole of the "catholic" world (33). But they further admit that "the tradition of icons is a later 'superstructure'" so that "In this way emphasis is given above all to the role of patristic tradition" (33–34). For the iconophiles, "the boundaries of tradition are boundaries set by the Apostles and the Fathers. That is to say, they identify the tradition of the Church with the teaching of the Fathers" (31). The guide for discerning between "orthodoxy" and "heresy" is not Scripture alone as separate from and above the later Church but rather the living tradition and practice of this Church itself as embodied in its privileged teachers, the Holy Fathers. Especially prominent among the citations from the Fathers (35–42) are passages from Athanasius of Alexandria's *Third Discourse against the Arians* 23.5 and Basil of Caesarea's *On the Holy Spirit* 18.45, in which it is affirmed that the honor given to an icon of the emperor passes on to the emperor himself (35–36). This is taken as justifying the veneration of images as a means by which appropriate honor is given to Christ and to the saints depicted in them. And other arguments are also given, such as purported miracles performed through icons (46–49).

With respect to the antiquity of their position, the iconoclasts arguably had a very strong case. In the first place, the citations from Athanasius and Basil do not establish a practice of venerating icons in their time – only that these figures recognized the "logic" behind the veneration of persons through images of them. Whether they would have considered it appropriate for Christians is another matter altogether. But on this point, one might also consider how Origen presents the Christian attitude toward images: "We clearly show the sacred character of our origin, and do not conceal it ... since even in people only just converted we inculcate a scorn of idols and all images, and in addition to this raise their thoughts from serving created things in the place of God and lift them up to the Creator of the universe" (*Against Celsus* 3.15). A bit later, he writes that "we take away from the deity worship by [images]" (3.34).

As a profoundly influential and representative figure of the "catholic" tradition such as it existed in that day, as one who had traveled to various portions of the Christian world before composing *Contra Celsum* as an old man, Origen apparently speaks as though the veneration of images was not only uncommon among Christians but also unheard of. But the iconoclasts could not have cited Origen authoritatively since he was nearly universally rejected as a heretic after the fifth ecumenical council or Constantinople II (553 CE). And, for the iconophiles, the appeal to tradition served not so much the purpose of demonstrating antiquity of opinion but rather to associate an opinion with the "confidence in the sacred persons who had handed it down" (Giakalis 2005: 23). This can be taken as an example of a case in which a concern for "orthodoxy" or "heresy" obstructs and imposes undue limits upon the theological pursuit of the truth. The veneration of images is most plausibly a novelty and development that did not exist in the most notable quarters of the "catholic" tradition from the beginning. The theological discussion about it should have treated it as such. But the evidence to establish this point would not have been admitted by one party because it comes from "heretical" sources (cf. Giakalis 2005: 24, 49–50).

In the opinion of Andrew Louth, "Among the defenders of icons and their veneration at the outbreak of iconoclasm, the most distinguished was Saint John Damascene" (Louth 2003: 9). Some of John's arguments for the iconophile position can be summarized here. With respect to the argument that God had forbidden the creation and worship of images, John responds that this was owing to the fact that the Hebrews had seen no form or likeness of God during their liberation from Egypt. God's purpose was to prevent them from worshiping the created order, something to which he considers the Jews to have been predisposed. But in the Incarnation God took upon Himself a visible, depictable form, so the prohibition no longer applies (*Treatises* 1.4–8). "Of old, God the incorporeal and formless was never depicted, but now that God has been seen in the flesh and has associated with human kind [*sic*], I depict what I have seen of God" (1.16, 2.14). He also distinguishes between the form of veneration that is proper to God from those more familiar modes of veneration that are offered to creatures. They are not the same act, so one can venerate the created while not offering that veneration that is due only to God (1.14). In addition, the practice of creating and venerating images is defended as an unwritten tradition of the Church (1.23, 2.16).

These arguments are interesting and have proven influential in the defense of the iconophile position throughout the ages. At the same time, it must be admitted that Leo III's question has no obvious answer. No one clear authority within the "catholic" tradition left the instruction that images be created and venerated in the church. The habit arose at some point and commended itself as a meaningful pious practice for many. The defense of this practice by the iconophiles would seem rather to be founded upon the authority of the church itself. The bishops at Nicaea II (787 CE) affirmed in their *Definition* that Christ "espoused to himself the Holy Catholic Church without spot or defect" and "promised that He would so preserve her." Moreover, this promise was made not only to the first disciples "but to us also who should believe in His name through their word."

And yet those bishops and others who had adopted the iconoclastic position are said to have "fallen from the right faith." These persons are described as priests, but "in name only, not in fact." Thus, it is not the past church as a whole, nor the present church as a whole, nor even the present church as an institutional body, but only this particular party within the church that (simply on its say-so?) has maintained its continuity and identity as the true "orthodox" church and has been preserved from the "heretical" error of iconoclasm.

In the controversy about images, one finds two competing visions for the authority of the teaching and practice of the contemporary church. The icono-clasts were willing to call into question an established convention and practice of their own time for the sake of greater faithfulness to an originating source. The presupposition of the iconoclast position is that the church and the Christian world can take a turn in the wrong direction without immediately knowing it (cf. Giakalis 2005: 22), so it later has to correct course. In the iconophiles, on the other hand, one is encountering a tradition that in a sense takes itself and its truth for granted. Even if one cannot specify by whom in particular or in what way, the tradition of making and venerating images has been left by "the Holy Fathers" apart from whom there is no "orthodox" faith. The iconophiles cannot conceive that their heroes in the faith could have been mistaken about this, because they do not conceive of the faith as something distinct and separable from these heroes. The thing itself (the faith) becomes inextricably connected to those who testify to it (the Holy Fathers).

3.4 The Real Presence

Christ taught that whoever does not eat His flesh and drink His blood does not have life (John 6:53–58). On the night of His betrayal, He took bread and wine, gave thanks for them, and distributed them to His disciples, saying: "Take, eat, this is my body; this is my blood; do this in remembrance of me" (Luke 22:19; 1 Cor. 11:24–25). And the apostle Paul teaches that the cup and the bread of the Lord's Supper are a sharing in the blood and body of Christ (*koinōnia estin tou haimatos / tou sōmatos tou Christou*; 1 Cor. 10:16). These are the central biblical *loci classici* for the theology of the Eucharist. A final example of the discernment of "orthodoxy" and "heresy" in Christian theological history concerns the manner in which Christ's body and blood are said to be "in" the bread and the wine of this sacrament.

A lively discussion on this subject began in the ninth century at the Benedictine abbey in Corbie, France. A monk named Paschasius Radbertus composed "the first known systematic treatise on the Eucharist in the history of theology" (Salkeld 2019: 60). He argued that the bread and wine truly were the body and blood of Christ, although they maintained their appearances as ordinary food "as a veil to protect the communicant from the horror of eating raw flesh" (60). This proved controversial for other theologians of the time, implying as it does both cannibalism and deception in the sacrament. By way of response to the controversy, the Frankish emperor Charles the Bald asked another monk named Ratramnus the fateful question: whether Christ is present in the sacrament "in figure or in truth" (61). Ratramnus's answer was that Christ is present in figure and not in truth. While this answer led to accusations that Ratramnus was denying the Real Presence of Christ in the Eucharist, Brett Salkeld notes that modern scholars reject this interpretation of what he said (61). He appears to have defined "truth" as what appears to the senses. Although Ratramnus maintained that there is a sacramental change of some sort during the celebration of the Eucharist, it is not perceptible. Thus, Ratramnus had to say that Christ was not present "in truth" – that is, perceptibly – but only "in figure."

At the turn of the millennium, a monk named Berengarius of Tours would take up Ratramnus's arguments (mistakenly thought by Berengarius as belonging to John Scotus Eriugena) against the exaggerated sacramental "realism" that had become predominant in his time (Salkeld 2019: 63). He argued that Christ could not be really present in the bread and wine because He was not perceptible there. He also argued that Christ could not truly say: "This [bread] is my body" unless the bread remained instead of being transformed into His body (64). In response to pressure from his theological opponents, Pope Nicholas II summoned Berengarius to Rome in 1059 CE, where he was forced to swear an oath drafted by Cardinal Humbert of Silva Candida. This oath is now known as *Ego Berengarius*, or "I Berengarius," after its opening words. In it the monk was made to swear that "the bread and wine which are placed on the altar are not merely a sacrament after consecration, but are rather the true body and blood of our Lord Jesus Christ – and that these are truly, physically [*sensualiter*] and not merely sacramentally, touched and broken by the hands of the priests and crushed by the teeth of the faithful" (65).

Salkeld notes that there are at least two problems with this oath (Salkeld 2019: 66). First, the adverb *sensualiter* wrongly makes Christ's presence an empirical or physical matter, undermining the sacramental nature of the presence. Second, the notion that Christ's body is "broken by the hands of the priests and crushed by the teeth of the faithful" seems problematic from the point of view of the impassibility or invulnerability of Christ's resurrected body. Berengarius then repudiated the oath upon returning to France and continued his polemics against it and the theology it represents. However, the theologian Lanfranc of Bec offered a critical response to Berengarius by appealing to the notion of "substance" (66–67). Whereas Berengarius could not conceive of a change in the bread and wine that would not be perceptible to the senses, Lanfranc insisted that in the Eucharist is a non-manifest change: the "substance" or "deepest reality" of the bread and wine becomes the body and blood of Christ while the appearances of bread and wine remain (67). Lanfranc thus utilizes the distinction between what a thing is and the way it manifests itself in order to make sense of the Real Presence of Christ's body and blood in the Eucharist.

Berengarius would argue against Lanfranc that the change of the substance of the bread and wine into the body and blood of Christ undermines the sacramental nature of the Eucharist. There is nothing left to be a "sacrament" or a sign (Salkeld 2019: 69). But he seems not to have convinced his opponents. He was once more summoned to Rome in 1079 CE and made to swear a second *Ego Berengarius*. This time it said: "I, Berengar, believe with my heart and confess with my mouth that the bread and wine which are placed on the altar are changed in their substance [*substantialiter converti*] into the true flesh and blood of Jesus Christ, by the Holy Prayer and the words of our Redeemer . . . and they are really this, not only by virtue of the sign and power of this sacrament, bur in their peculiar nature and their substantial reality" (69–70). Berengarius himself was not entirely satisfied by this oath. But the specification of the mode of the presence of Christ's body and blood in the bread and wine as substantial – which is to say, purely ontological and non-manifest – seems to have brought the debate to an end (70).

Although its origins are uncertain, the term "transubstantiation" appears in the next century. It even finds its way into the pronouncement of the Fourth Lateran Council (1215 CE) against the Cathars and Albigensians that "only duly ordained priests can consecrate the Eucharist" (Salkeld 2019: 71). This council does not define the term rigorously or precisely but uses it simply in order to assert the Real Presence (Salkeld 2019: 36). "Transubstantiation" as a term made it possible to speak about the distinctly sacramental mode of Christ's Real Presence in the bread and wine of the eucharistic meal. It avoided "spiritualizing" the Eucharist by asserting an ontological change in the elements while also insisting on the non-physical or non-manifest nature of the change so as to avoid the implication of cannibalism (Salkeld 2019: 72).

The historically most significant statement of transubstantiation comes from Thomas Aquinas in the thirteenth century. In *Summa Theologiae* 3.75–77 he addresses several questions regarding the proper understanding of transubstantiation. Thomas teaches that Christ is really present in the sacrament and not only by signification, taking Berengarius to have been first person to have denied this (3.75.1). Christ is present not because the substance of the bread and wine is annihilated but rather because it is changed or "transubstantiated" into the substance of His body and blood (3.75.3). This change takes place purely by the power of God and cannot otherwise be explained (3.75.4). Even so, the appearances of bread and wine remain by God's providence in order that believers and non-believers alike not be horrified at the eating of flesh and blood, as well as so that those who partake might be rewarded for their faith in what cannot be seen (3.75.5). At the same time, Christ's body is present in the sacrament "after the manner of substance" (*secundum modum substantiae*) and not locally (3.76.5). The mode of presence is not local or spatial, which would make it empirical. Neither is the presence in the sacrament of such a nature as to allow Christ to be affected or "moved" by what happens to the sacramental species (3.76.6). And because the substance of Christ's body and blood is present in the sacrament in a way that is entirely unmanifest to the senses, it can be "perceived" by the intellect alone (3.76.7). It is a non-manifest ontological presence of the sort proposed by Lanfranc.

The essential elements of this understanding of things were in large part endorsed by the Council of Trent in its "Decree concerning the Most Holy Sacrament of the Eucharist" (1551 CE). It confirmed that "in the august sacrament of the holy Eucharist, after the consecration of the bread and wine, our Lord Jesus Christ, true God and man, is truly, really, and substantially contained under the species of those sensible things" (Waterworth 1848: 76). He is made present because "by the consecration of the bread and the wine, a conversion is made of the whole substance of the bread into the substance of Christ our Lord, and of the whole substance of the wine into the substance of His blood; which conversion is, by the holy Catholic Church, suitably and properly called Transubstantiation" (78). Finally, various anathemas are pronounced against erroneous beliefs, such as the opinion that Christ is present in the Eucharist only "as in a sign, or in figure, or in virtue" (83).

Not only the doctrine of transubstantiation but the understanding of the Eucharist in general became a significant point of controversy during the Reformation (see the essays in Wandel 2014). Roman Catholics and Protestants engaged in persistent debates about whether and how Christ can be said to be present in the celebration of the Eucharist. A number of theories were developed and proposed that continue to be the topic of discussion for theologians (see especially Arcadi 2016, 2019, 2021). Even so, some modern theologians are convinced that there may be more common ground among Protestant, Roman Catholic, and Eastern Orthodox iterations of the Real Presence tradition than previous generations may have appreciated (Hunsinger 2008; Salkeld 2019).

The following observation about the evolution of "orthodoxy" and "heresy" in Christian theology can be made by way of conclusion. The debates between Berengarius and Lanfranc led to the specification of the purely ontological and non-manifest mode by which the bread and wine are changed and Christ becomes present in the sacrament. When seen in comparison to the preceding history of theology in the church, this specification also brings into sharp relief the fact that the developing "orthodoxy" of the "catholic" tradition had for a very long time been principally concerned with the proper formulation of ideas about realities purportedly lying beyond the reach of the senses and natural reason.

The anti-Gnostic polemic of Irenaeus called for a turn to the things of experience through the comparative-hermeneutical argumentation for the apostolic tradition from Scripture as well as from verifiable recent church history. The Gnostics were wrong because their interpretations of Scripture could be seen by any attentive reader to be inadequate to the texts themselves. Not only that, one could in principle attend any of the churches founded by the apostles themselves and find there a succession of teachers who have never known anything like what the Gnostics claimed to teach.

The preoccupations of the "catholic" tradition are then turned away from the world of experience to the sphere of pure thought with the trinitarian debates of the fourth century. There was a felt need for a struggle to find precisely the right formula for making sense of the utterly unique relation that obtains between Father, Son, and Holy Spirit, one that has no proper analog or corollary in the world of natural human experience. To this end the purely ontological term "consubstantial" or *homoousios* eventually seemed most satisfactory. And the pure mystery of the "orthodox" teaching was well appreciated by John of Damascus: "[T]he manner in which [God is trinity] is beyond manner, for God is incomprehensible. Do not ask how the Trinity is Trinity, for the Trinity is inscrutable" (*On Heresies* 103; cf. Rahner 1970: 50).

In the controversy about images, the "catholic" tradition, which to that point had won so many battles against "heresies," asserted itself once more with the assistance of imperial powers. Its mode of reasoning in this case essentially affirmed its own infallibility. The practice of the creation and veneration of images was received as part and parcel of the "orthodox" faith passed down by the "Holy Fathers." It did not matter that the practice plainly was not universal from the beginning, nor that it could not provide a concrete answer to Leo III's question: "Tell me, whoever taught us to venerate and revere images made by human hands?" (Giakalis 2005: 23). It suffices that it is now the practice and opinion of so many respected members of the "orthodox" church, which understands itself to have been promised divine guidance and protection from error by Christ. Rather than seeing the church in history as subordinate and accountable to an originating revelation (Scripture) outside of itself as the iconoclasts did, the "orthodox" party does not separate the revelation to which it is accountable from the living church in all times as embodied in the practice and teaching of its "Holy Fathers."

Finally, when confronted with an apparent contradiction between the manifest world and its liturgical discourse, between the appearances of bread and wine and the announced body and blood of Christ, the "catholic" tradition once more places the object of its concern beyond the "screen" of appearance. In its eucharistic doctrine it does not speak about what is manifest but rather subordinates the manifest to something unmanifest. The bread becomes the body of Christ. He is present while remaining unmanifest, invisible, imperceptible, unseen. As in the case of images, the "catholic" tradition does this out of an attempt to be true to its inherited faith, indeed to what it takes to be the unanimous testimony of its forebears to the Real Presence of Christ in the bread and wine (cf. Salkeld 2019: 57). In its opinion, the "first deviser" of the "heresy" that Christ is present in the meal by signification alone was Berengarius (Thomas Aquinas, *ST* 3.75.1). And it is hard not to see a connection between these two aspects. Precisely because what "orthodoxy" teaches concerns realities beyond the natural reach of the human being, its only mode of access and demonstration is by appeal to testimony, specifically the authorized testimony of the tradition of this church and its preferred representatives. In this way, the theological "thing itself" becomes inseparable from the persons testifying to it.

4 Scripture and Tradition

It has become evident at this point in the discussion that the question of "orthodoxy" and "heresy" in Christian theology is closely related to the question of the relationship between scripture and tradition as sources and authorities for Christian belief and practice. There are considerable differences on these matters between Protestants, Roman Catholics, and Eastern Orthodox in the present day. The purpose of the present section is briefly to survey some of the most common opinions offered by thinkers from these various communities.

On one hand, the tendency on the side of Protestant theologians is to emphasize the priority of scripture as uniquely canonical and infallible in relation to all ecclesial traditions. The tendency on the side of the Roman Catholic and Eastern Orthodox thinkers, on the other hand, is to call attention to the fact that scripture arose from within the prior context of the tradition of the community of God's people, with reference to which it must be interpreted if it is to be understood correctly. Both of these perspectives have something of the truth, but they are also incomplete. This section therefore terminates with a synthesis of these two ideas, according to which scripture and tradition exist in a relation of mutual or reciprocal priority to one another: tradition is formally and phenomenologically prior to scripture, whereas scripture is materially and theologically prior to every particular ecclesial tradition.

4.1 Scripture First

The typical Protestant position is that scripture retains priority over every tradition. In the words of Oliver Crisp, it is the *principium theologiae* or "beginning of theology" and *norma normans non normata*: the absolute standard that measures everything else (Crisp 2009: 17–20). At the same time, it is clear that the interpretation of scripture is often controverted. This raises the question of ecclesial tradition and its role in the interpretation of the Bible.

On this issue Protestants disagree. All agree that ecclesial tradition is penultimate, but there may be differences of emphasis among them. Crisp accepts the primacy and ultimacy of scripture while at the same time underlining that a theologian ignores or disregards the ecumenical councils and authoritative theologians of the past at his or her own peril (Crisp 2009: 17–20). These sources have enough weight that they ought not be ignored or lightly set aside. For Kevin Vanhoozer (2005, 2016), on the other hand, scripture relates to the church in the way a theatrical script relates to an acting troupe. The traditions of the church are simply fallible "performances" of the script of scripture. These may be more or less true to the intention of the divine playwright, by which the quality of each performance is ultimately judged. Indeed, it is a part of the tradition of the church precisely that Scripture enjoys this status of primacy and ultimacy (Vanhoozer 2005: ch. 5). Thus, Cyril of Jerusalem: "Do not believe me merely because I tell you these things, unless you receive from the inspired Scriptures the proof of the assertions" (*Catechetical Lectures* 4.17).

In roughly the same spirit, John Peckham argues that scripture alone is intrinsically canonical as a guide for the covenant community of God. The texts are not canonical because the community uses them as such, but rather they are canonical because God intends them for this purpose (2016: ch. 1). Peckham is skeptical of the value of positing further canons for theology beyond the inspired texts themselves, such as the believing community or the "rule of faith" or the tradition of the church. First, there are many such communities or "rules" or ecclesial traditions from which to choose. Second, these extrabiblical canons are themselves also the subjects of hermeneutical and interpretive disputes (chs. 5–6). Thus, he argues that the task of interpreting scripture is not made easier by positing further interpretable and ambiguous guides for interpretation.

4.2 Ecclesial Tradition First

Whereas the typical Protestant position emphasizes the priority of scripture to ecclesial tradition, the Roman Catholic and Eastern Orthodox position is more often to emphasize the priority of the living tradition of the community as the context within which scripture arose and with reference to which it ought to be interpreted.

The position of Eastern Orthodox theologians is unanimously that scripture arose from within the context of the community of God's people and must be interpreted in keeping with this community (Florovsky 1972; Breck 2001; Humphrey 2013). John Anthony McGuckin writes that the Bible is "constitutively within sacred tradition, not apart from it" (2008: 101). Roman Catholic theologians likewise agree with this point. Gerald O'Collins writes that "The Bible nowhere declares its autonomy, as if it had supplanted tradition, the very force that brought it into existence" (2011: 198). And he says elsewhere that "understood either as the active process (*actus tradendi*) or as the object handed on (the *traditum*), tradition [*traditio*] includes Scripture rather than simply standing alongside it" (215; cf. O'Collins 2018). At the same time, while agreeing with the Eastern Orthodox about the situation of scripture within the community, Roman Catholic theology also gives a more definite answer to the way in which the church's authoritative interpretation of scripture is discerned.

The question of the relation of scripture and ecclesial tradition was raised at the Second Vatican Council (1962–1965). In the "Dogmatic Constitution on Divine Revelation" (*Dei Verbum*), the Catholic Church teaches that the saving revelation of Jesus is passed down by the apostles through their preaching and especially through their inspired writings. This preaching is preserved by "an unending succession of preachers," especially those who "have received through Episcopal succession the sure gift of truth" (*DV* 8). In this way, the understanding of this revelation grows over time, although the task of authoritatively interpreting scripture is reserved only for "the living teaching office of the Church," which at the same time is thought of as "not above the word of God but [in service to] it" (*DV* 10).

In the "Dogmatic Constitution on the Church" (*Lumen Gentium*), the bishops as the successors of the apostles are appointed by Jesus to be "shepherds in His church even to the consummation of the ages" (*LG* 18). It is through the bishops that the apostolic tradition is manifested to the world until the present day (*LG* 20). The bishops, together with the presbyters and deacons, "preside in the place of God over the flock" (*LG* 20). Indeed, through their consecration to the episcopacy, bishops are given a special charism of the Holy Spirit by which they are specially empowered to perform their task (*LG* 21). Principal among these bishops is the bishop of Rome, with whom the other bishops must maintain communion as their head (*LG* 22). And among other things, the bishops are empowered by God to teach infallibly under certain specified conditions: first, when in communion with one another and with the bishop of Rome they happen to agree in their teaching upon some matter of faith and morals as essential; second, when gathered together in an ecumenical council in order to define some matter of faith or morals (*LG* 25). In addition to these cases, the bishop of Rome specifically enjoys the charism of infallibility when he proposes to define some matter of faith or morals from his authority (*ex cathedra*) as the supreme teacher of the whole Church (*LG* 25; cf. *Pastor Aeternus* 4.9).

4.3 A Synthesis

Both of these perspectives have something of the truth but are also incomplete. It is necessary to distinguish two senses of priority. Ecclesial tradition is prior to scripture in a formal and phenomenological sense, whereas scripture is prior to every tradition of the church in a material and theological sense (Nemes 2022).

The Roman Catholic and Eastern Orthodox position is correct to say that scripture arose from within the context of a particular community and thus must be interpreted in light of that community. In other words, tradition is formally prior to scripture. Scripture is an attempted communication of the early church. And to understand what someone is trying to communicate, one must understand his or her words just as he or she does (cf. Vanhoozer 1998). Scripture can only be utterly unintelligible to the person who does not understand what the community means by "God," "Jesus," "salvation," "righteousness," "Israel," "judgment," and the like. This is what the formal priority of tradition amounts to.

It is also true to say that tradition is phenomenologically prior to scripture in the sense that every person who reads Scripture does so in light of the religious education he or she has received at the hands of others (White 2017: 35;

Nemes 2020: 76–78). Just as no one can see without sight, and each person sees only as well as his or her eyesight allows, so no one can read scripture without or apart from the enabling initiation into a tradition that supplies the preconceptions and presuppositions necessary to make sense of the biblical text (Heidegger 1996: 142–143; Gadamer 2013: 279–280). This is what it means to say that tradition is phenomenologically prior to scripture.

At the same time, these are only formal and phenomenological senses in which tradition is prior to scripture. They do not say anything concrete about the actual content of scripture. Scripture must be interpreted in light of the early community, but from this it does not follow that scripture must be read through the teaching of this or that particular contemporary community. Likewise, scripture cannot be read except through the lens of some tradition or other, but from this it does not follow that any particular tradition is the one by which scripture must be read. Every community must establish the theological identity and continuity of its own tradition with the tradition of the primordial group that produced scripture. But how can it do so? Only by competitive hermeneutics: by interpreting the text in a way that seems more natural than the interpretations of other comunities or traditions, as though its reading had come from the authors themselves. These considerations thus reveal the sense in which scripture is materially or theologically prior to every ecclesial tradition.

The goal of the reader of scripture is generally not merely to adopt a particular tradition and to see what sense it can make of the text. It is rather to understand what scripture has to say about God, the world, the human being, and so on. The text is *magister* and the reader *discipulus*. It is true that no one can read scripture at all apart from the enabling mediation of some tradition. But one can often find oneself being "pulled up short by the text" (Gadamer 2013: 280). One becomes aware that one's presuppositions and preconceptions are inadequate for making sense of the text. In that case, one is free to abandon these presuppositions and to search for others that will prove more illuminating. This is what the material and theological priority of scripture means.

Consider how a physical object is only perceptible from some point of view or other. There is no "view from nowhere." And every point of view makes visible and invisible, revealing some aspects of the object and possibly conceal-ing other aspects (cf. Elliot 2017). Suppose one is interested in some particular aspect of an object. If it is not visible from where one stands now, one can change one's perspective by moving someplace else. In so doing, one seeks that precise point of view from which the aspect in question can come into clear light (cf. Merleau-Ponty 2014: 315–316). So also with Scripture and tradition, which relate to each other like object and perspective. Every tradition provides a set of definitions and prior conceptions that make it possible to assign meaning to the text. But these are only valuable to the extent that they manage to shed light on what scripture means to say. If one tradition proves inadequate to this task, it can be adjusted or traded for another.

It would therefore seem most adequate to say that scripture and tradition exist in a relationship of mutual or reciprocal priority. Tradition is prior to scripture in a formal and phenomenological sense. Scripture itself is the product of the tradition of the earliest church and must be read in light of it. Indeed, one cannot read scripture at all except from the point of view of some tradition or other. At the same time, the goal of the scriptural reader is to understand what scripture itself says. Conceding these formal and phenomenological senses of priority still proves nothing regarding the actual teaching of scripture. Every contemporary church or tradition must demonstrate its theological identity and continuity with that primordial tradition of the church by demonstrating that it best of all makes it possible to understand scripture. And if one tradition shows itself inadequate to the task in this respect, it can always be adjusted or replaced with another.

5 Theology without Anathemas

To this point, the discussion has addressed the formal analysis of the concepts of "orthodoxy" and "heresy," the material discernment of "orthodoxy" and "heresy" as much in the Old and New Testaments as also in the history of the theology of the church, and the question of the relationship between scripture and ecclesial tradition as sources and authorities for Christian theology. The purpose of this concluding section is to present a critique of the notions of "orthodoxy" and "heresy" and to argue instead for a Christian theology "without anathemas" (cf. Nemes 2021a, 2021b). The argument draws on an analogy with the dispute between phenomenological and representationalist conceptions of consciousness. Essentially, the point is that the "catholic" tradition, precisely because of its preoccupation with matters of "orthodoxy" and "heresy," obeys a certain "logic" that compromises it epistemically.

5.1 Philosophical Prelude

The critique begins with the Aristotelian definition of truth. Aristotle wrote: "To say of what is that it is not, or of what is not that it is, is false, whereas to say of what is that it is, or of what is not that it is not, is true" (*Metaphysics* 1011b25). This definition proposes truth as a relation of adequacy between what is thought or said about a thing and that thing itself. At the same time, it suggests that thought and speech are in an important way independent of what is thought or spoken about. Only if a thing can be independently of what is thought or said about it is the distinction between truth and falsity possible.

In order to think or to speak about something, it is necessary that this something be given in some way to the person thinking or speaking. This givenness takes place in conscious experience (Husserl 1973: 19). As Edmund Husserl said: "Every type of object that is to be the object of a rational proposition, of a prescientific and then of a scientific cognition, must manifest itself in knowledge, thus in consciousness itself, and it must permit being brought to givenness, in accord with the sense of all knowledge" (1965: 90). Consciousness is how the thinking and speaking individual is put into lived contact with the things about which he or she might wish to think or speak.

Importantly, in the phenomenological tradition, experience is not arbitrarily limited to sensible intuition by means of the five senses but includes every originary mode by which objects are given to consciousness (Marion 2008: 56–57). The world of experience thus includes not only sensible objects but also, for example, the truths of geometry and mathematics (Henry 2012: 70–71). And, phenomenologically speaking, the "world" is nothing other than this milieu or horizon of visibility in which things manifest themselves to consciousness in varying degrees of clarity or obscurity (70).

If truth is a matter of thinking or speaking adequately about things as they are, then one can define "knowledge" as being aware that one is thinking or speaking adequately about things. But truth is a relation between what is thought or said about a thing and that thing itself. And the awareness of a relation between two things is not possible unless both related items are given (cf. Nemes 2019: 212). For example, one cannot see that one cat is fatter than another unless both are presented. In the same way, one cannot see that $x > 100$ unless the value of x is given. This is because the awareness of a relation is a comparison of two items and comparison presupposes that the comparanda are given. It is impossible to compare what is given with what is not. From this it follows that it is impossible to be aware that one is in possession of the truth – that is, that one thinks or speaks adequately about a thing as it is, so long as the thing itself about which one has an opinion is not manifest. The thing itself would not be given for comparison with one's thought or speech.

From these considerations follows a certain method for inquiry. If one wishes to ascertain the truth of an opinion about something, one must turn to the thing itself in experience and compare it with the opinion in question. The truth of thought or speech about a thing is confirmed by means of the thing itself. The principle for truthful inquiry is thus to allow the thing itself to dictate the terms in which it is understood (Husserl 1965: 102).

Such a method presupposes that the world of conscious experience is the domain in which the things themselves about which one thinks or speaks are revealed. But this conception of consciousness is not universally accepted. There is a significant representationalist tradition according to which what are given in consciousness are not the things themselves but rather "representations" or "images" that arise as a result of the strictly unmanifest interaction of one's body with its surrounding physical environment (cf. Zahavi 2017: 187ff.). What appears in consciousness is not the thing itself but a representation that may or may not correspond to anything real. A fundamental rupture is thus posited in principle between manifestation and being.

But the phenomenological tradition objects to representationalism on the grounds that it leads to skepticism and an "egocentric predicament" (Sokolowski 2000: 9–11; Schindler 2013: 6). It becomes impossible to escape the purely subjective "theater" of consciousness in order to determine whether one's "representations" are adequate to the things themselves of which one takes them to be representations. Any determination would have to take place in an experience the representational adequacy of which is already in question. The representationalist rejoinder to this problem is to posit certain "feelings of certainty" or "feelings of evidence" that take place immanently in consciousness and serve as signals that one is in the possession of the truth (Heidegger 1985: 50).

The phenomenological response is that one can have feelings of certainty about virtually anything, so "any reference to them is useless as a criterion or even definition of truth" (Zahavi 2003: 32). This is especially evident whenever one goes from being convinced about the truth of some proposition to being convinced of its falsity in some matter the truth of which could not have changed in the meantime – for example, in matters of metaphysics, ethics, or history. At most, one could only insist dogmatically that one is in possession of the truth while simultaneously admitting one's inability to prove it noncircularly. The phenomenological tradition therefore insists that knowledge as the awareness of the truthfulness of one's thought or speech demands a strict correlation between being and manifestation, between what is and what appears.

The truth of one's thinking or speaking about a thing therefore must be judged in comparison with the thing itself, and this comparison can take place only in experience. Put another way, knowledge as consciously truthful thought or speech is possible only if the known thing is "accessible." Representationalism, on the other hand, follows what may be called a "logic of the inaccessible." The logic is as follows. One is concerned to possess knowledge about a thing. But the thing itself is non-manifest and inaccessible in experience. One only experiences images that perhaps represent it. Therefore, one posits "signals" that are themselves manifest and accessible and through which one can be confident that one is in possession of knowledge.

At the same time, this logic is critically unstable. Representationalism grants that the domain of the manifest and the domain of real being are distinct from each other and possibly non-correlated. What appears may not be real, and what is real may not appear. The two are distinct onto-epistemological spheres. Thus, the correlation between any manifest "signal" and the reality of one's desired object of knowledge is a contingent and accidental one at best. Any inference from the manifest presence of the signal to the real thing will therefore be circular or a strict non sequitur.

The phenomenological method for rational inquiry is consequently to call for a return "to the thing itself" in experience. One ought to think and speak about things precisely as they manifest themselves in experience. At the same time, however, this process is inevitably fallible and subject to revision. Two arguments may be given for this conclusion here.

First, in every experience of a thing, one is always in the position of choosing between two possible interpretations of what is given. One may say that the given thing is X, or one may say that the given thing is not actually but only presently resembles something that is X. A person in a crowd may be one's friend, or else he or she may only presently resemble one's friend. It is of course possible that future experiences will disconfirm one or the other judgment. But even then one is in the position of choosing between thinking that the person really is (or is not) one's friend or else that the person is not really but only has until now persistently seemed (or not) to be one's friend. This fact of the persistent multiple interpretability of experience thus makes one's knowledge of things apart from oneself as they are revealed in experience to be essentially fallible and subject to revision in principle.

Second, the relation to things in experience does not occur directly but only as a result of the simultaneous "cooperation" of a number of factors. On one hand, the way a thing appears is at least in part a result of everything else that is present in its environment. For example, a person's body may be obscured by the desk at which he or she is sitting, or by the lack of light in the place where he or she is located, and so on. On the other hand, the way a thing appears is also at least in part a result of the way one is. A person in the distance looks blurry, not because he or she is blurry, but because one's eyesight is poor. Food may taste bad or good depending on whether one is in health or sickness. A word or phrase may seem offensive, not because one's interlocutor means to offend, but because one is sensitive or insecure. Thus, a thing seems the way it does not only because of the way it is but also because of the way everything else is, oneself included. And because one cannot step outside oneself to determine the adequacy of one's grasp of a thing, it follows that the knowledge one has of things by way of experience is essentially fallible and subject to revision in principle.

5.2 Critique of "Catholicism"

On the basis of these formal considerations about rational inquiry and method, it is possible to offer a critique of "orthodoxy" and "heresy" as essential aspects of the theological method of the "catholic" tradition.

The analyses of Section 1.1 revealed that judgments of "orthodoxy" and "heresy" presuppose a background framework of thought to which one is antecedently committed. An idea is "orthodox" or "heretical" only relative to other ideas the "orthodoxy" or "canonicity" of which is taken for granted. The denial of the Real Presence is "heretical," for example, at least in part because it is incompatible with the judgment that the authoritative figures in the tradition of the church unanimously affirmed it, and these cannot all have erred. In this sense, "orthodoxy" and "heresy" are a matter of "horizontal" relations between ideas.

But ideas are first and foremost about things. And the Aristotelian dictum teaches that the truth of an idea is a matter of its adequacy to its object. It is a "vertical" relation of the idea to the thing itself. Thus, if theology is to be concerned with the truth so defined, considerations of "orthodoxy" and "heresy" must be considered strictly irrelevant (compare Pannenberg 1991: ch. 1). The relationship of one idea to other ideas is unrelated to whether it is adequate to its object. Alternatively, to the extent that theology is principally concerned with "orthodoxy" and "heresy," it becomes less a matter of truth in the Aristotelian sense and more a matter of the propagation and development of a particular system of ideas. It loses its grounding in the things it purports to talk about and gets caught up with its own ideas about them.

The "catholic" tradition certainly maintains that its ideas are both "orthodox" and true. But to prove them as such is not easy. The historical survey of Section 3 made clear that this tradition developed in such a way as to locate the objects of its "orthodox" beliefs outside the sphere of the manifest. Thomas would come to argue explicitly that theology or sacred doctrine is concerned with "a teaching revealed by God beyond the philosophical disciplines, which are investigated by human reason" (*ST* 1.1.1). In other words, theology is different from the other fields of inquiry made possible given the natural endowments of the human being, such as physics, chemistry, biology, history, ethics, and the like. These are concerned with the "accessible," with what manifests itself in the world of experience, whereas theology for the "catholic" tradition is concerned with what is "inaccessible" and non-manifest. Thus, to the extent that it wishes to assert the truth of its ideas about these non-manifest realities, it will be forced to follow the "logic of the inaccessible" and posit certain "signals" by which one can be assured of the truth. And this is in fact what happens.

The more the "catholic" tradition finds the truth of its opinions impossible to establish on the basis of what is manifest, the more it leans on "signals" by which its possession of the truth is purportedly guaranteed. Thus, Vincent of Lérins proposes a rule by which one can "distinguish the truth of catholic faith from the falsehood of heretical pravity" in spite of the multiple interpretability and ambiguity of scripture at the hands of the "heretics" (*Commonitorium* 4–5; cf. Guarino 2013). This is the rule of universality, antiquity, and consent. One must believe that which is affirmed by the whole of the church, in keeping with the famous teachings of the holy ancestors and fathers, according to the definitions and determinations of all or at least most of the priests and doctors (*Commonitorium* 6). The truth of the "catholic" faith is antecedently inaccessible because scripture is ambiguous, so one must find it by the "signals" of universality, antiquity, and consent. But this rule is either useless or circular. Who is included in the "Church"? Who counts as a "holy ancestor and father"? If "heretical" opinions and figures are not excluded a priori, then there is hardly any substantial theological opinion will satisfy these rules.

On the other hand, if one begins with particular preconceptions regarding the extent of the "Church" and who constitutes a "holy ancestor," then the answers are predetermined from the start. One has done no more than to establish the "catholic truth" of one's own opinions by assuming a framework within which they are "catholic." But worst of all is the fact that the truth *sensu stricto* has gone untouched in all this. Once more, truth is a matter of the adequacy of what is thought or said about a thing with that thing itself. But when it is a question of the truth, Vincent's rule does not give the thing itself but only further authorized opinions and commentators on the thing. The Aristotelian dictum presupposes that a thing is what it is independently of anyone thinks or says about it. Speech and being are distinct spheres only contingently and accidentally correlated. Only thus is the distinction between truth and falsehood possible. Thus, Vincent's rule cannot serve the purpose of guaranteeing the truth. It falls into the instability of the "logic of the inaccessible." It is at best a rule for preserving a particular tradition or complex of ideas to which one antecedently belongs.

It should be noted here that the argument is not necessarily that anything the authorities of the "catholic" tradition assert is false. This would be next to impossible to prove, since this tradition intentionally speaks about what lies beyond the manifest world of experience and thus beyond the possibility of verification or disconfirmation. At best one can show that its ideas are inconsonant with other ideas one might find plausible. But the "catholic" can always retort that revelation trumps human intuition and mere plausibility. The argument here is rather that the "catholic" theological tradition is epistemically compromised to the extent that it depends upon a "logic of the inaccessible."

This "catholic" tradition attempts to overcome its epistemological difficulties by appeal to the activity of the Holy Spirit in creating a privileged class of interpreters. In various ways, these are arguments for the possibility of infallibility in theology. The Protestant doctrine of *claritas Scripturae* or "the perspicuity of Scripture," for example, teaches that the Holy Spirit enlightens all truly regenerate readers of the Bible so that they cannot fail to grasp the essential contours of the Gospel in its pages (Vanhoozer 2016: 112–113). But no matter what "signal" one posits by which the truly regenerate reader of the Bible is identified, one will find multiple persons who disagree as to what the essential contours of the Gospel really are. And if one proposes only those "signals" by which one is distinguished from one's theological opponents, then one has set oneself up in sectarian fashion as a "signal" of the truth of one's own opinions, which is circular and self-serving (Nemes 2021a: 189; cf. Berger 1998: 35).

On the other hand, Roman Catholic doctrine asserts that the teaching magisterium is divinely guided and especially protected from error when it exercises its teaching authority in certain conditions, as mentioned in Section 4.2 (*LG* 25; *DV* 8–10; *PA* 4.9; Sullivan 1983; Dulles 2017). But this presupposes a certain conception of apostolic succession that is without an adequate basis either in scripture or in the early history of the church. It assumes that the power of binding and loosing inherited from the apostles implies a certain infallibility belonging to the position of bishop as such (cf. Matt. 16:19, 18:18; Ott 1954: 287).

This point is eminently disputable (Nemes 2021a: 190; 2021b: 39–46). In Irenaeus, there is nothing about the office of presbyter/bishop that implies any divine protection from error or special guidance into the truth, as was noted earlier (cf. *AH* 3.3.1, 4.26.3). And in Tertullian, what makes the churches founded in his day "apostolic" is not that their bishops can in principle trace their ordination by means of other bishops back to an apostle – a possibility he and Irenaeus do not mention at all and that seems to play no role in their thinking – but rather the fact that they accept the apostolic teaching (*Prescription against the Heretics* 32). The only succession that counts is one of teaching. Thus, if later generations of bishops come to claim this gift of infallibility for themselves, it is hard to avoid the conclusion that they do so (knowingly, unknowingly) out of a desire to make their pronouncements unquestionable, not because they can be demonstrated with reference to the things themselves, but simply because they are the ones making them (Nemes 2021a: 190–191). They too set themselves up as "signals" of the inaccessible truths of their theological opinions, which is circular.

What is being argued here is that the conditions and limitations of human knowledge are the same in theology as in other fields. Theology is merely one more way for human beings to put into practice their natural capacities for rational inquiry. There is no "special" theological epistemology. But some philosophers and theologians deny this. Kevin Diller (2014) argues for a special theological epistemology by synthesizing insights from Karl Barth and Alvin Plantinga. From Barth, he gets the notion that theological knowledge is a gift received from God the possession of which surpasses the power of human nature to obtain for itself. From Plantinga, he gets the epistemological framework within which to make sense of how this gift of knowledge is received.

Diller is obviously following the "logic of the inaccessible." Theological knowledge for him is the "inaccessible" that is received only as a gift. And the "signal" is what Diller following Plantinga calls "doxastic perception," by which a person comes to perceive the truth of some theological proposition by the help of the Holy Spirit (Diller 2014: 148). This perception is not a verification of the truth of some theological sentence by comparison with the thing to which it refers. One does not come by the help of the Holy Spirit to see the truth of the sentence "Christ is Lord" through a direct experience of Christ Himself. Rather, one "perceives the truth" of the proposition simply because one finds oneself with a strong inclination to believe it even apart from a direct experience of the thing itself to which the proposition refers (cf. Diller 2014: 149). Diller thus appears to do no more than posit the "feelings of evidence" of the representationalist tradition. But one can have such feelings about anything at all, regardless of whether one's opinions are in fact true. Therefore, Diller's proposal does not succeed in showing how a "special" theological epistemology can succeed (Nemes 2017: 207–209, 211–214).

In fact, there is a more significant critique to make here. Suppose one admits the definition of theology as a science concerned with non-manifest realities that lie beyond the boundaries of the world of experience as made accessible by the natural faculties of the human being. How else could one conceive of special theological knowledge except as Diller as done? One must speak of "perceiving" because only thus can one refer to a direct experience worthy of the title of "knowledge." But such knowledge must consist in "perceiving the truth" of a theological proposition apart from any experience of the theological realities to which the proposition itself refers, because these are inaccessible *ex hypothesi*. And because the powers of human nature are limited to what manifests itself in the world made accessible by these very powers, the possession of theological knowledge that targets objects beyond the world is attributed to divine assistance (Diller 2014: 157).

One finds exactly this dialectic in Thomas: "Because those things which are of faith surpass human reason, hence they do not come to man's knowledge, unless God reveals them" (*ST* 2–2.6.1). But there is no "perceiving the truth" of a theological proposition apart from the experience of the things themselves to which the proposition refers. As Aristotle teaches, truth is a relation between what is thought or said about a thing and that thing itself, and there is no perceiving a relation in the absence of one of the relata. Moreover, the attempt to posit "signals" by which one can know that one is in possession of theological knowledge means falling into the instability of the "logic of the inaccessible." The "signal" one posits will not signal infallibly. Thus, the project of a "special" theological epistemology seems doomed to failure.

The alternative is to admit that theology is subject to the same limiting conditions as any other field of rational inquiry. This means that the only criteria for determining the truth of what it says are or at least ought to be the things themselves about which it speaks. For example, if one speaks about a biblical text, then the biblical text alone is the standard for one's speech about it, just as if one speaks about a figure from church history, that figure alone is the standard for one's speech about him. And because access to these things is fallible, so also are the opinions of theologians who attempt to think or speak about them. There is no infallibility in theology. This is not to say that there is no truth in theology but only that the grasp of the truth is as uncertain as in other fields. And it seems obvious that there is no room for ideological notions of "orthodoxy," "heresy," and "anathemas" in a field whose single principle of inquiry is not the coherent propagation and expansion of received ideas but rather (fallibly) to describe things as truly and accurately as possible.

The distinctly theological notion of the "anathema" arises from within a framework in which "orthodoxy" and "heresy" are of central concern. The formal "anathema" is the means by which the "orthodox" community purifies itself of "heresy," expressing and formalizing its determination not to live-with those who are judged "heretical" in their beliefs-that or ways of living-with God and the community. The "anathema" is a means for the clarification and self-preservation of "orthodoxy." The critique of the concern for "orthodoxy" and "heresy" as relations between ideas therefore carries consequences for the practice of anathematization. In this way, the critique of the "catholic" tradition leads to a theology "without anathemas."

5.3 Theology "without Anathemas"

By way of conclusion, it would be well to sketch the contours of a theology "without anathemas" as an alternative to "catholic" theology by noting the consequences of the preceding argument. First, theology "without anathemas" essentially differs from "catholic" theology only in method and not necessarily in any of its conclusions. It does not concern itself with "orthodoxy" and "heresy," it does not pronounce "anathemas," and it does not pretend to be infallible. It is only concerned with truth. It allows no other standard of its statements except the things themselves which it purports to study. It does not claim to have come across "final" answers on this side of the *eschaton* (Pannenberg 1991: ch. 1; Kärkkäinen 2013: ch. 1; Peckham 2016). But even so, the theologian "without anathemas" does not necessarily reject the doctrines of the Trinity, Incarnation, and other such, so long as he or she considers these doctrines to be truest to the things themselves, such as they appear.

Second, theology "without anathemas" follows from the recognition of the fallibility of theological beliefs-that. But because belief-that is fallible and subject to revision in principle, it would seem inadequate to serve as a criterion of salvation or of community in the church. The so-called Athanasian Creed or *Quicunque vult* famously does exactly this. It says: "Whosoever wishes to be saved, before everything it is necessary that he hold the catholic faith" (Schaff 1877: 66). This "catholic" faith is then elaborated as a series of metaphysical statements about the consubstantiality of Father, Son, and Holy Spirit as well as about the two natures of Christ (Schaff 1877: 66–70). The Creed concludes by saying that unless a person believes all this faithfully, "he cannot be saved" (Schaff 1877: 70). But these opinions are fallible. One cannot be sure they are right. To make them conditions of salvation is therefore to invite constant salvation anxiety (Nemes 2021b: 49). For this reason, theology "without anathemas" does not condition salvation on the assent to very particular beliefs-that.

Third, theology "without anathemas" prioritizes belief-in over belief-that (Nemes 2021a: 193–196; 2021b: 49–50). It says that what makes a person to be a Christian is not his or her particular beliefs-that but rather the fact that he or she believes-in Jesus. A person's beliefs-that are a result of the way things seem to him or her, and the way anything seems to him or her is a result not only of the way everything else is at that time but also of the way he or she is. Put another way, beliefs-that are a result of contextually particular factors. Consider the following analogy.

The shape and size of a tree are a result of a number of contextual factors: how much sunlight and rain it receives, whether it is surrounded by other trees, whether animals live in it, whether its branches are pruned, and so on. Even so, it grows toward the sun all the same simply because that is what it is to be a tree. In the same way, Christian belief-in Jesus is a matter of growing toward Him, whatever the more precise details of the theoretical context in which this takes place. This means that the "orthodox" and the "heretics" are (or are not)

Christians to the extent that they believe-in and "grow toward" Jesus (or not), regardless of what their beliefs-that might be and even apart from their willingness (or not) to live-with one another.

Fourth, theology "without anathemas" emphasizes the sacrifice of Jesus as the basis for confident Christian theological investigation. Belief-that is not a condition of salvation because it is essentially fallible. On the other hand, belief-in Jesus is a response to His own prior demonstration of His trustworthiness. Christ has died for the sins of the whole world and calls all persons to friendship with Him and His Father (cf. 2 Cor. 5:19–21; 1 Tim. 2:4–6). The truth about every person is that he or she is one for whom Christ died. Theological investigation thus need not be racked by salvation anxiety nor obsessively preoccupied with infallibility. Christ has died for all. Consider how scientists of differing opinions and points of view are concerned with the one and the same world that they investigate together and that provides a home for all of them alike. In the same way, the common "world" that all Christians inhabit, which has space enough for all of them together and with which they are concerned in their theological investigations, is the "world" of God's saving intervention through Jesus Christ.

Fifth and finally, theology "without anathemas" opens up the possibility of rethinking the things of Christianity as located within the manifest world of experience. The phenomenologist Michel Henry (2003, 2012, 2015) has already taken the first significant steps toward this project from a purely philosophical perspective. Some from within the broader "catholic" tradition have objected to Henry on this score (Rivera 2015; see also Nemes 2021d). Even so, the theologian "without anathemas" may find in Henry's philosophy a tremendous resource for a restatement of the content of Christian faith from within the domain of the manifest (Nemes 2021c; cf. Behr 2019). This would be a theological statement of the Christian faith that does not depend upon the "logic of the inaccessible" and does not commit itself to the pretensions of the "catholic" tradition more generally. But such a fuller restatement of Christianity as an interpretation of the manifest world of experience remains as a project to be pursued in greater detail in the future.

A person first confronted with the notion of a "theology without anathemas" might immediately think of Paul's "anathema" against those who preach "another gospel" in Gal. 1:8–9. If Paul could do this, why shouldn't the practice of anathematization be permissible or even necessary at times in the present day? By way of response, one could first note that it is not clear that Paul is in fact offering a formal "anathema" rather than simply engaging in extreme rhetoric. But it is also worth noting that the case is not the same in later theology. The Gentiles had received the Holy Spirit, proof that God had chosen them, and yet were told that they had to submit to circumcision in order to be proper members of the people of God's Messiah. There was an empirical disproof of the alternative position at hand, and Paul does not hesitate to use it (Gal. 3:2–3). But there is no such disproof at hand in the case of the purely theoretical and speculative-metaphysical questions debated in the history of Christian "orthodoxy." The difference in subject matter thus demands a different approach because of the difference in the availability and interpretability of the evidence.

The lesson in brief is this. "Orthodoxy" and "heresy" have to do with the relations between ideas, whereas truth is a relation of an idea to the thing itself of which it is the idea. Against the "catholic" tradition, theology "without anathemas" does not concern itself with considerations of "orthodoxy" and "heresy" but only with thinking and speaking truthfully about things. One allows only the things themselves to serve as the standards and "canon" of what one thinks and says. One does this because one believes-in Jesus who died for the sins of the whole world, with whom one wishes to live, and who is one's principal object of investigation. And precisely because one does not pretend to possess a special knowledge of the things about which one thinks and speaks, one does not "anathematize" or purify oneself of "heresy" but rather invites to a sober and calm conversation in which the things themselves alone are canonical.

References

Anatolios, Khaled (2011). *Retrieving Nicaea: The Development and Meaning of Trinitarian Doctrine*. Grand Rapids, MI: Baker Academic.

Arcadi, James M. (2016). Recent Philosophical Work on the Eucharist. *Philosophy Compass* **11**(7), 402–412.

(2019). *An Incarnational Model of the Eucharist*. New York: Cambridge University Press.

(2021). On the Intelligibility of Eucharistic Doctrine(s) in Analytic Theology. In James M. Arcadi and James T. Turner, eds., *The T & T Clark Handbook of Analytic Theology*. New York: T & T Clark, 463–476.

Aristotle (2009). *The Nicomachean Ethics*, David Ross, trans. New York: Oxford University Press.

(2016). *Metaphysics*. C. D. C. Reeve, trans. Indianapolis, IN: Hackett.

Athanasius (1971). *Contra Gentes and De Incarnatione*. Robert W. Thomson, trans. Oxford: Clarendon.

Ayres, Lewis (2004). *Nicaea and Its Legacy: An Approach to Fourth-Century Trinitarian Theology*. New York: Oxford University Press.

Barth, Karl (1956). *Church Dogmatics. Volume 4: The Doctrine of Reconciliation, Part I*. Geoffrey W. Bromiley, trans. London: T & T Clark.

Bauer, Walter (1971). *Orthodoxy and Heresy in Earliest Christianity*. Robert A. Kraft, trans. Philadelphia: Fortress Press.

Behr, John (2001). *The Formation of Christian Theology*, vol. 1: The Way to Nicaea. Crestwood, NY: St. Vladimir's Seminary Press.

(2004). *The Formation of Christian Theology*, vol. 2: The Nicene Faith, 2 parts. Crestwood, NY: St. Vladimir's Seminary Press.

(2019). *John the Theologian and His Paschal Gospel: A Prologue to Theology*, New York: Oxford University Press.

Berger, Michael S. (1998). *Rabbinic Authority*. New York: Oxford University Press.

Breck, John (2001). *Scripture in Tradition: The Bible and Its Interpretation in the Orthodox Church*. Crestwood, NY: St. Vladimir's Seminary Press.

Crisp, Oliver D. (2009). *God Incarnate: Explorations in Christology*. New York: T & T Clark.

Cyril of Jerusalem (1968). *The Works of Saint Cyril of Jerusalem*, vol. 1. Leo P. McCauley, SJ, and Anthony A. Stephenson, trans. Washington, DC: Catholic University of America Press.

Dalley, Stephanie (2009). *Myths from Mesopotamia: Creation, the Flood, Gilgamesh, and Others*. New York: Oxford University Press.

Diller, Kevin (2014). *Theology's Epistemological Dilemma: How Karl Barth and Alvin Plantinga Provide a Unified Response.* Downers Grove, IL: IVP Academic.

Dulles, Avery, Cardinal (2017). *Magisterium: Teacher and Guardian of the Faith.* Ave Maria: Sapientia.

Edwards, Mark (2009). *Catholicity and Heresy in the Early Church.* Burlington, VT: Ashgate.

Elliot, Robert (2017). Givenness and Hermeneutics: The Saturated Phenomenon and Historically-Effected Consciousness. *Heythrop Journal* **58**(4), 662–677.

Eno, Robert (1990). *The Rise of the Papacy.* Wilmington, DE: Michael Glazier.

Flavius Josephus (1998). *The Complete Works.* William Whiston, trans. Nashville, TN: Thomas Nelson.

Florovsky, Georges (1972). *Bible, Church, Tradition: An Eastern Orthodox View.* Belmont, MA: Nordland.

Gadamer, Hans-Georg (2013). *Truth and Method.* Joel Weinsheimmer and Donald G. Marshall, trans. New York: Bloomsbury.

Giakalis, Ambrosios (2005). *Images of the Divine: The Theology of Icons at the Seventh Ecumenical Council*, revised edition. Boston: Brill.

Goldin, Shmuel (2008). *Unlocking the Torah Text: An In-Depth Journey into the Weekly Parsha-Shmot.* New York: Oxford University Press.

Goldingay, John (2014). *The Theology of the Book of Isaiah.* Downers Grove, IL: IVP Academic.

Guarino, Thomas G. (2013). *Vincent of Lérins and the Development of Christian Doctrine.* Grand Rapids, MI: Baker Academic.

Hartog, Paul A., ed. (2015). *Orthodoxy and Heresy in Early Christian Contexts: Reconsidering the Bauer Thesis.* Cambridge: James Clarke & Company.

Heidegger, Martin (1985). *History of the Concept of Time: Prolegomena*, Theodore Kisiel, trans., Bloomington: Indiana University Press.

(1996). *Being and Time.* Joan Stambaugh, trans. Albany: State University of New York Press.

Henry, Michel (2003). *I Am the Truth: Toward a Philosophy of Christianity.* Susan Emanuel, trans. Stanford, CA: Stanford University Press.

(2012). *Words of Christ.* Christina M. Gschwandtner, trans. Grand Rapids, MI: Eerdmans.

(2015). *Incarnation: A Philosophy of Flesh.* Karl Hefty, trans. Evanston, IL: Northwestern University Press.

Heschel, Abraham Joshua (1955). *God in Search of Man: A Philosophy of Judaism.* New York: Harper Torchbooks.

Husserl, Edmund (1965). *Phenomenology and the Crisis of Philosophy.* Quentin Lauer, trans. New York: Harper & Row.

(1973). *Experience and Judgment: Investigations in a Genealogy of Logic.* James S. Churchill and Karl Ameriks, trans. Evanston, IL: Northwestern University Press.

Holmes, Michael W. (2007). *The Apostolic Fathers: Greek Texts and English Translations of Their Writings.* 3rd edition. Grand Rapids, MI: Baker Academic.

Humphrey, Edith M. (2013). *Scripture and Tradition: What the Bible Really Says.* Grand Rapids, MI: Baker Academic.

Hunsinger, George (2008). *The Eucharist and Ecumenism: Let Us Keep the Feast.* New York: Cambridge University Press.

John of Damascus (1958). *Writings* Frederic H. Chase Jr., trans. Washington, DC: Catholic University of America Press.

(2003). *Three Treatises on the Divine Images.* Andrew Louth, trans. Crestwood, NY: St. Vladimir's Seminary Press.

Kärkkäinen, Veli-Matti (2013). *Christ and Reconciliation.* Grand Rapids, MI: Eerdmans.

Kelly, John N. D. (1968). *Early Christian Doctrines.* London: Adam & Charles Black.

Köstenberger, Andres J., and Michael J. Kruger (2010). *The Heresy of Orthodoxy: How Contemporary Culture's Fascination with Diversity Reshaped Our Understanding of Early Christianity.* Wheaton, IL: Crossway.

Lampe, Peter (2003). *From Paul to Valentinus: Christians at Rome in the First Two Centuries.* Michael Steinhauser, trans. Minneapolis, MN: Fortress Press.

Latinovic, Vladimir (2017). Arius Conservativus? The Question of Arius' Theological Belonging. In Markus Vinzent, ed., *Studia Patristica* **95**, 27–41. Bristol: Peeters.

Levenson, Jon D. (1994). *Creation and the Persistence of Evil: The Jewish Drama of Divine Omnipotence.* Princeton, NJ: Princeton University Press.

Liddell, Henry George, and Robert Scott (1996). *A Greek–English Lexicon*, revised edition. Oxford: Clarendon.

Louth, Andrew (2003). Introduction. In St. John of Damascus, *Three Treatises on the Divine Images.* Andrew Louth, trans. Crestwood, NY: St. Vladimir's Seminary Press.

Maccoby, Hyam (1988). *Early Rabbinic Writings.* New York: Cambridge University Press.

Mansoor, Menahem (2007). Pharisees. In Fred Skolnik and Michael Berenbaum, eds., *Encyclopedia Judaica. Volume 16: Pes-Qu.* 2nd edition. New York: Thomson Gale.

Marion, Jean-Luc (2008). *The Visible and the Revealed.* Christina M. Gschwandtner, trans. New York: Fordham University Press.

McGuckin, John Anthony (2008). *The Orthodox Church: An Introduction to Its History, Doctrine, and Spiritual Culture.* Malden, MA: Blackwell.

Merleau-Ponty, Maurice (2014). *Phenomenology of Perception.* Donald A. Landes, trans. New York: Routledge.

Middleton, J. Richard (2005). *The Liberating Image: The* Imago Dei *in Genesis 1.* Grand Rapids, MI: Brazos.

Nemes, Steven (2016). Christian *Apokatastasis*: Two Paradigmatic Objections. *Journal of Analytic Theology* **4**, 66–86.

(2019). *Claritas Scripturae*, Theological Epistemology, and the Phenomenology of Christian Faith. *Journal of Analytic Theology* **7**, 129–218.

(2020). On Reading the Bible as Scripture, Encountering the Church. *Perichoresis* **18**(5), 67–86.

(2021a). Theology without Anathemas. *Journal of Analytic Theology* **9**, 180–200.

(2021b). Against Infallibility. *Criswell Theological Review* **19**, 27–50.

(2022b). Michel Henry and the Prospect of a Christian Spiritual Inactivism. *Journal of Spiritual Formation and Soul Care* **15**(1), 92–114. http://doi.org/10.1177/19397909211036144.

(2021d). The Life-Idealism of Michel Henry. *Journal of French and Francophone Philosophy*, **29**(1–2), 87–108.

(2022a). Can analytic theology be phenomenological? Forthcoming in *Journal of Analytic Theology.*

O'Collins, Gerald (2011). *Rethinking Fundamental Theology.* New York: Oxford University Press.

(2018). *Tradition: Understanding Christian Tradition.* New York: Oxford Univesity Press.

Origen (1953). *Contra Celsum*, Henry Chadwick, trans. New York: Cambridge University Press.

(2017). *On First Principles.* 2 vols. John Behr, trans. New York: Oxford University Press.

Osborn, Eric (2001). *Irenaeus of Lyons*, New York: Cambridge University Press.

Ott, Ludwig (1954). *Fundamentals of Catholic Dogma*, Patrick Lynch, trans. Fort Collins, CO: Roman Catholic Press.

Pannenberg, Wolfhart (1991). *Systematic Theology*, vol. 1. Geoffrey W. Bromiley, trans. Grand Rapids, MI: Eerdmans.

Peckham, John C. (2016). *Canonical Theology: The Biblical Canon*, Sola Scriptura, *and Theological Method*. Grand Rapids, MI: Eerdmans.

Pelikan, Jaroslav Jan (1971). *The Christian Tradition: A History of the Development of Doctrine. Volume 1: The Emergence of the Catholic Tradition (100–600)*. Chicago: University of Chicago Press.

Rahner, Karl (1970). *The Trinity*, Joseph Donceel, trans. New York: Continuum.

Ratzinger, Joseph Cardinal (2004). *Introduction to Christianity*. J. R. Foster, trans. San Fransisco: Ignatius.

Rivera, Joseph A. (2015). *The Contemplative Self after Michel Henry: A Phenomenological Theology*. Notre Dame, IN: Notre Dame University Press.

Salkeld, Brett (2019). *Transubstantiation: Theology, History, and Christian Unity*. Grand Rapids, MI: Baker Academic.

Schaff, Philip (1877). *Creeds of Christendom with a History and Critical Notes. Volume II: Greek and Latin Creeds, with Translations*. New York: Harper & Brothers.

Schindler, David C. (2013). *The Catholicity of Reason*. Grand Rapids, MI: Eerdmans.

Singer, Isidore, ed. (1906). *The Jewish Encyclopedia*, vol. 3. New York: Funk & Wagnalls.

Sokolowski, Robert (2000). *Introduction to Phenomenology*. New York: Cambridge University Press.

Sommer, Benjamin D. (2015). *Revelation and Authority: Sinai in Jewish Scripture and Tradition*. New Haven, CT: Yale University Press.

Stewart, Alistair C. (2014). *The Original Bishops: Office and Order in the First Christian Communities*. Grand Rapids, MI: Baker Academic.

Sullivan, Francis A. (1983). *Magisterium: Teaching Authority in the Catholic Church*. Eugene, OR: Wipf & Stock.

(2001). *From Apostles to Bishops: The Development of the Episcopacy*. New York: Newman Press.

Swinburne, Richard (2007). *Revelation: From Metaphor to Analogy*. New York: Oxford University Press.

Tertullian (1914). *On the Testimony of the Soul and the "Prescription" of Heretics*, T. Herbert Bindley, trans. SPCK.

Torrance, Thomas F. (1991). *The Trinitarian Faith: The Evangelical Theology of the Ancient Catholic Church*. London: T&T Clark.

(2016). *The Christian Doctrine of God, One Being Three Persons*. New York: Bloomsbury.

Turner, David L. (2008). *Matthew*. Grand Rapids, MI: Baker Academic.

Vanhoozer, Kevin J. (1998). *Is There a Meaning in This Text? The Bible, the Reader, and the Morality of Literary Knowledge*. Grand Rapids, MI: Zondervan.

(2005). *The Drama of Doctrine: A Canonical-Linguistic Approach to Christian Doctrine*. Louisville, KY: Westminster John Knox Press.

(2016). *Biblical Authority after Babel: Retrieving the* Solas *in the Spirit of Mere Protestant Christianity*. Grand Rapids, MI: Brazos Press.

Wandel, Lee Palmer, ed. (2014). *A Companion to the Eucharist in the Reformation*. Boston: Brill.

Waterworth, James (1848). *The Canons and Decrees of the Sacred and Œcumenical Council of Trent*. London: C. Dolman.

White, Thomas Joseph (2017). *The Light of Christ: An Introduction to Catholicism*. Washington, DC: Catholic University of America Press.

Zahavi, Dan (2003). *Husserl's Phenomenology*. Stanford, CA: Stanford University Press.

(2017). *Husserl's Legacy: Phenomenology, Metaphysics, and Transcendental Philosophy*. New York: Oxford University Press.

Cambridge Elements ≡

The Problems of God

Series Editor
Michael L. Peterson
Asbury Theological Seminary

Michael Peterson is Professor of Philosophy at Asbury Theological Seminary. He is the author of *God and Evil* (Routledge); *Monotheism, Suffering, and Evil* (Cambridge University Press); *With All Your Mind* (University of Notre Dame Press); *C. S. Lewis and the Christian Worldview* (Oxford University Press); *Evil and the Christian God* (Baker Book House); and *Philosophy of Education: Issues and Options* (Intervarsity Press). He is co-author of *Reason and Religious Belief* (Oxford University Press); *Science, Evolution, and Religion: A Debate about Atheism and Theism* (Oxford University Press); and *Biology, Religion, and Philosophy* (Cambridge University Press). He is editor of *The Problem of Evil: Selected Readings* (University of Notre Dame Press). He is co-editor of Philosophy of Religion: Selected Readings (Oxford University Press) and *Contemporary Debates in Philosophy of Religion* (Wiley-Blackwell). He served as General Editor of the Blackwell monograph series Exploring Philosophy of Religion and is founding Managing Editor of the journal *Faith and Philosophy*.

About the Series
This series explores problems related to God, such as the human quest for God or gods, contemplation of God, and critique and rejection of God. Concise, authoritative volumes in this series will reflect the methods of a variety of disciplines, including philosophy of religion, theology, religious studies, and sociology.

Cambridge Elements ☰

The Problems of God

Elements in the Series

Divine Guidance: Moral Attraction in Action
Paul K. Moser

God, Salvation, and the Problem of Spacetime
Emily Qureshi-Hurst

Orthodoxy and Heresy
Steven Nemes

Printed in the United States
by Baker & Taylor Publisher Services